GCSE
Religious Studies:
Philosophy and Applied Ethics
for OCR B
Revision Guide

HODDER
EDUCATION
AN HACHETTE UK COMPANY

Cover photo © Rubberball/Jupiter Images

Scripture taken from the New International Version of the Holy Bible. Copyright
© 1973, 1978, 1984 by International Bible Society.

Every effort has been made to trace all copyright holders, but if any have been
inadvertently overlooked the Publishers will be pleased to make the necessary
arrangements at the first opportunity.

Although every effort has been made to ensure that website addresses are correct at
time of going to press, Hodder Education cannot be held responsible for the content of
any website mentioned in this book. It is sometimes possible to find a relocated web
page by typing in the address of the home page for a website in the URL window of
your browser.

Hachette UK's policy is to use papers that are natural, renewable and recyclable
products and made from wood grown in sustainable forests. The logging and
manufacturing processes are expected to conform to the environmental regulations of
the country of origin.

Orders: please contact Bookpoint Ltd, 130 Milton Park, Abingdon, Oxon OX14 4SB.
Telephone: +44 (0)1235 827720. Fax: +44 (0)1235 400454. Lines are open
9.00a.m.–5.00p.m., Monday to Saturday, with a 24-hour message answering service.
Visit our website at www.hoddereducation.co.uk

© Jon Mayled 2010
First published in 2010 by
Hodder Education
Carmelite House
50 Victoria Embankment
London EC4Y 0DZ

Impression number   11
Year   2017

Typeset in 11/13pt Usherwood Book by Gray Publishing, Tunbridge Wells
Printed in India

A catalogue record for this title is available from the British Library

ISBN 978 1 444 11071 5

Contents

Introduction

How to use this guide

The aim of this guide is to help you revise and improve your exam skills so that you attain your highest possible performance in GCSE Religious Studies.

You should read the section below on exam techniques first so that you know what types of questions are asked by OCR and what sorts of answers are expected. If you are taking the short-course examination you should then work through each of the four topics you are studying. If you are sitting the full-course examination then you should work through the eight topics you are studying. Some of you may have studied extra topics as well.

Each topic is divided into sections which you should use in the following way:

- Learn the key words for the section.
- Learn the key facts and main facts for the section.
- Learn the key people associated with the section so that you can show how they are relevant to the question.
- Learn the key texts for the section so that you can refer to them to show your understanding of how they apply to the question.

At the end of this book there are some practice questions. Try these and check your answers against the full-mark answers to see how well you have done. Remember, there may be different ways of answering the questions which are equally good.

If your answers show that you are having problems:

- Check whether your problem is that you cannot remember the facts. If it is, relearn the appropriate section.
- Check whether your problem is that you have not answered (or addressed the focus of) the question properly. If it is, reread the exam techniques section below.

Exam techniques
Techniques for choosing questions

Each exam paper is divided into three topics. You will have studied at least two of these. In each topic there is a choice of six questions, one on each of six religions.

Each question is in five parts. You should only answer one question from each topic that you have studied.

All the questions have the following parts:

(a) 1 mark for knowledge
(b) 2 marks for knowledge
(c) 3 marks for knowledge
(d) 6 marks for understanding
(e) 12 marks for evaluation.

Remember! You have to do a complete question — this means you must answer parts (a), (b), (c), (d) and (e) from the same question.

Types of questions
Part (a) questions

These are short-answer knowledge questions, for example, 'What is abortion?'. You do not need to write full sentences for your answers. These questions often ask for the meanings of the key words.

Part (b) questions

These are short-answer knowledge questions, which may require a one- or two-sentence answer.

Part (c) questions

These may ask for three pieces of information or ask for a description.

Part (d) questions

These are all understanding questions and usually begin with the word 'explain'.

You should go through the question and highlight the key words that tell you how to write your answer:

- 'Why' means you should use the word 'because' and give reasons. For example: 'Explain why many Christians are opposed to divorce' means you should answer in a way such as 'Many Christians are against divorce because they believe that the marriage vows are between the couple and God as well as each other ...' (you would then go on and give any more reasons you can think of).
- 'How' means you should connect ideas. For example, 'Explain how the teachings of Christianity might be used to help overcome prejudice' means you should write out some teachings and then explain how they could help Christians to overcome prejudice.
- Explain why there are different attitudes means you must identify viewpoints and explain why people have these. For example, 'Explain why Christians might have different attitudes to the role of women in worship' means give reasons why some Christians think women cannot be priests or lead worship, then give reasons why some Christians think women can be priests and leaders.

For marking part (d) and (e) questions examiners use grids which show the marks for the level of response which is in the answer. Opposite is the grid for part (d) questions which are marked out of six. From this you can see what you need to do in your answer to get higher marks.

Levels of response for marking AO1 part (d) questions

Level 0 0 marks	No evidence submitted or response does not address the question.
Level 1 1–2 marks	A weak attempt to answer the question. Candidates will demonstrate little understanding of the question. • A small amount of relevant information may be included. • Answers may be in the form of a list with little or no description/explanation/analysis. • There will be little or no use of specialist terms. • Answers may be ambiguous or disorganised. • Errors of grammar, punctuation and spelling may be intrusive.
Level 2 3–4 marks	A satisfactory answer to the question. Candidates will demonstrate some understanding of the question. • Information will be relevant but may lack specific detail. • There will be some description/explanation/analysis although this may not be fully developed. • The information will be presented for the most part in a structured format. • Some use of specialist terms, although these may not always be used appropriately. • There may be errors in spelling, grammar and punctuation.
Level 3 5–6 marks	A good answer to the question. Candidates will demonstrate a clear understanding of the question. • A fairly complete and full description/explanation/analysis. • A comprehensive account of the range and depth of relevant material. • The information will be presented in a structured format. • There will be significant, appropriate and correct use of specialist terms. • There will be few, if any errors, in spelling, grammar and punctuation.

Part (e) questions

These are evaluation questions. They begin with a statement in quotation marks and then ask you to discuss this statement. You should include different, supported points of view and a personal viewpoint. You must refer to Christianity in your answer.

The question asks you to discuss the statement. You should:

- look at a Christian view and say, with reasons, why people have this view
- look at another Christian view or the view of another religion or a secular view and say, with reasons, why people have this view
- state your own view and say, with reasons, why you have this view.

You will not gain above Level 2 if you do not give a personal view. Of course, your personal view may be the same as one of the views you have already given but you must still explain it and say why you think in this way.

Opposite is the grid for part (e) questions which are marked out of twelve. From this you can see what you need to do in your answer to get higher marks.

Levels of response for marking AO2 part (e) questions

Level 0 0 marks	No evidence submitted or response does not address the question.
Level 1 1–3 marks	A weak attempt to answer the question. Candidates will demonstrate little understanding of the question. <ul><li>Answers may be simplistic with little or no relevant information.</li><li>Viewpoints may not be supported or appropriate.</li><li>Answers may be ambiguous or disorganised.</li><li>There will be little or no use of specialist terms.</li><li>Errors of grammar, punctuation and spelling may be intrusive.</li></ul>
Level 2 4–6 marks	A limited answer to the question. Candidates will demonstrate some understanding of the question. <ul><li>Some information will be relevant, although may lack specific detail.</li><li>Only one view might be offered and developed.</li><li>Viewpoints might be stated and supported with limited argument/discussion.</li><li>The information will show some organisation.</li><li>Reference to the religion studied may be vague.</li><li>Some use of specialist terms, although these may not always be used appropriately.</li><li>There may be errors in spelling, grammar and punctuation.</li></ul>
Level 3 7–9 marks	A competent answer to the question. Candidates will demonstrate a sound understanding of the question. <ul><li>Selection of relevant material with appropriate development.</li><li>Evidence of appropriate personal response.</li><li>Justified arguments/different points of view supported by some discussion.</li><li>The information will be presented in a structured format.</li><li>Some appropriate reference to the religion studied.</li><li>Specialist terms will be used appropriately and for the most part correctly.</li><li>There may be occasional errors in spelling, grammar and punctuation.</li></ul>
Level 4 10–12 marks	A good answer to the question. Candidates will demonstrate a clear understanding of the question. <ul><li>Answers will reflect the significance of the issue(s) raised.</li><li>Clear evidence of an appropriate personal response, fully supported.</li><li>A range of points of view supported by justified arguments/discussion.</li><li>The information will be presented in a clear and organised way.</li><li>Clear reference to the religion studied.</li><li>Specialist terms will be used appropriately and correctly.</li><li>Few, if any errors, in spelling, grammar and punctuation.</li></ul>

1.1 Beliefs about the nature of God 1

Christians believe that God is made of three parts or 'persons'. This is called the Trinity. This means that there are three ways of God being God:

- God who is Father – the transcendent creator.
- God who is Son – Jesus who is immanent and personal, who came to earth and lived a human life.
- God who is Holy Spirit – immanent, but impersonal, the way God inspires and guides Christians every day.

Main facts

- People find it very difficult to say what God is like because God is beyond human understanding. When people talk about God they tend to use pictures, symbols or symbolic language to describe God.
- Sometimes people describe God by saying what God is 'not' like: for example, God is not jealous, God is not cruel.
- The writers of the Bible often used images: God is called a shepherd, a warrior, a judge, a king, a father and even a mother hen.
- However, these are human images, and so can limit God as God is not a human being or an animal, and to say that he is makes him less than God. This way of explaining God is called anthropomorphism.

Key words

Immanent: God is within all.
Transcendent: God is above all.

Remember

The Trinity shows that there are three different ways of thinking about God. It does not say that there are three gods.

1.2 Beliefs about the nature of God 2

God's 'nature' means his characteristics, his attributes, his qualities. Christians believe in one God – they are monotheists. Christians say that God is difficult to describe, but they do believe that he has certain characteristics.

Main facts

- God's 'nature' means his characteristics, his attributes, his qualities.
- God is outside time and space, he is transcendent and eternal.
- God is omnipotent (all-powerful), and omniscient (all-knowing).
- God is omnibenevolent (all-good and all-loving); this means he wants the best for people and gives them rules to live by.
- God will judge everyone.
- God created the universe for a purpose.

Key words

Analogy: using a word symbolically to suggest something else.
Monotheists: people who believe in one God, such as Christians, Jews, Muslims.
Myth: a story which is not factually true, but which has important spiritual truths.
Symbol: a way of explaining the unexplainable, and using something to represent something else.
Omnibenevolence: all-good.
Omnipotent: all-important.
Omnipresent: all-present.
Omniscient: all-knowing.

Key person

Julian of Norwich
(1342–c.1416) – a Christian hermit who wrote *The Revelations of Divine Love*

Remember

Jesus referred to God as 'Father', and in Christianity, God is called 'Father' in quite a literal sense: besides being the creator and nurturer of creation, and the provider for his children; the Father is said to have an eternal relationship to his only son, Jesus. However, God can also be seen as female and in *The Revelations of Divine Love*, St Julian of Norwich refers to God as a mother. This idea is also found in Isaiah.

Key texts

Genesis 1:26–27 – God made humans in his own image
Genesis 3:8 – God walking in the garden
Isaiah 66:13a – God as a mother
Matthew 11:27 – Jesus is the Son of God

1.3 Reasons given in support of belief

There are several different arguments that attempt to prove the existence of God which people have developed over 1000 years. Some are more convincing than others.

Main facts

- The ontological argument: God is 'That than which nothing greater can be conceived'. We cannot think of anything greater than God and therefore God exists.
- The cosmological argument: the universe must have come from somewhere – Christians believe it came from God. God is the 'First Cause'.
- The teleological argument: the world shows that it has been designed and so must have been created or designed by someone.
- The argument from experience: people can experience God which proves he exists. This may, for example, be through miracles, conversion, answered prayers or the numinous.
- The moral argument: people have a basic understanding of 'good' and 'bad', 'right' and 'wrong' and this knowledge must have come from God.

Key words

Big Bang theory: scientific theory which suggests that there was a massive explosion about 18 billion years ago and that this led to the creation of the whole universe.

Intelligent design: a theory which says that life is so complex that it must have been designed by a higher intelligent being, and did not evolve by natural selection.

Natural selection: theory that tiny differences and genetic mutations between creatures of the same species can sometimes make one individual slightly better suited to their environment than others. This means that it survives longer and has more offspring who inherit that trait.

Necessary being: theory of Thomas Aquinas that God must exist because he cannot not exist.

Numinous: a mysterious power that suggests the presence of a spirit or god.

Key people

St Anselm of Canterbury (1033–1109) – Archbishop of Canterbury from 1093 to 1109 who first put forward the ontological argument

St Thomas Aquinas (1225–74) – a philosopher and theologian who devised several versions of the cosmological argument

Isaac Newton (1642–1727) – a mathematician and one of the first people to propose the design argument

William Paley (1743–1805) – a clergyman who explained the design argument using the example of a watch

Charles Darwin (1809–82) – a naturalist who developed the theory of natural selection

Rudolf Otto (1869–1937) – a Christian theologian who wrote about the idea of the numinous

Remember

It is not always easy to explain beliefs, but it is important to challenge them in order to see how well they stand up, and to look for the flaws in the arguments both for and against belief in God.

Key text

On the Origin of Species by Means of Natural Selection or the Preservation of Favoured Races in the Struggle for Life – Charles Darwin's 1859 book in which he developed the theory of natural selection

1.4 Other views about belief in God

Arguments against God's existence would say that if God is in control why did he make us imperfect and incomplete in some way? Why not just make us perfect the first time, instead of us struggling to reach perfection? God cannot be all-good and all-powerful as Christians say because evil exists and he does nothing about it. They would also argue that there is no need of God for people to be moral and to make good moral decisions.

Main facts

Statements about the existence of God:
- If there is a God, whence proceed so many evils? If there is no God, whence cometh any good? (Boethius).
- If God did not exist, it would be necessary to invent him (Voltaire).
- A God who let us prove his existence would be an idol (Dietrich Bonhoeffer).
- 'The question, "How can you believe in a God who permits suffering on this scale?" is therefore very much around at the moment, and it would be surprising if it weren't – indeed it would be wrong if it weren't'. (Rowan Williams – Archbishop of Canterbury speaking after the 2004 Asian tsunami).

Key people

Boethius (c.480–524) – an early Christian philosopher
Voltaire (1694–1778) – a French philosopher
Dietrich Bonhoeffer (1906–45) – a German Lutheran minister
Richard Dawkins (1941–) – a modern scientist who is also a committed atheist
Rowan Williams (1950–) – Archbishop of Canterbury

Key words

Agnostic: somebody who believes that it is impossible to know whether or not God exist.
Atheist: someone who does not believe in God.

Remember

Many people would say that faith is blind and not rational: God was once the explanation for things we did not understand, but now it is God who needs explaining.

1.5 The concept of miracles

Miracles are not optional extras to Christianity. Indeed, Christianity is founded on miracles which are the beliefs that God became human (incarnation) and that he has power over death, shown in the resurrection of Jesus Christ.

Scientific laws can be looked on as reflecting the orderly and regular ways God works: the 'customs of God'. However, if God wishes to act differently for a particular purpose, and perform a miracle, Christians believe that he is free to do things differently.

Main facts

A miracle is:

* Something out of the ordinary that catches the attention.
* Intended by God as a sign of his love and/or power.
* A marvellous event which cannot have been brought about by humans or by nature and so is said to be performed by God.
* Something that usually shows control over the laws of nature such as a dead person being brought back to life.

Key words

Laws of nature: scientific generalisations arrived at by experimentation and/or observation, which try to explain how nature works, or how scientists expect nature to work.
Miracle: a marvellous event which cannot have been brought about by humans or by natural means.

Key person

Bernadette Soubirous (1844–79) – a young girl who saw eighteen apparitions of the Virgin Mary in 1858 at Lourdes, France

Remember

Many people are said to have recovered from illnesses after visiting Lourdes in France where, in 1858, Bernadette Soubirous had visions of the Virgin Mary. Many Christians go on pilgrimages to places such as Lourdes in the hope of physical and/or spiritual healing.

1.6 God intervening in the world through: miracles, Jesus and the Holy Spirit

God coming to earth as Jesus of Nazareth, both fully human and fully divine, is seen as one of the greatest miracles, as is Jesus' resurrection from the dead after the crucifixion.

Main facts

- Miracles are 'those things done by divine power apart from the order usually followed in things' (Thomas Aquinas). This can include:
  - those things that God does that nature cannot do, e.g. God stopping the sun in the sky
  - those acts that God does that nature could do, but not in the same order, e.g. someone recovering from a terminal illness
  - those things done by God that nature could do, but that God does without using the forces of nature, e.g. someone who quickly recovers from an illness after prayer.
- Jesus performed many miracles of different types:
  - healing miracles, e.g. the healing of the paralytic (Matthew 9:1–8)
  - nature miracles, e.g. calming the storm (Mark 4:35–41)
  - exorcisms, e.g. the healing of Legion (Mark 5:1–15)
  - raising people from the dead, e.g. Lazarus (John 11:1–44).
- Many miracles are seen as the work of the Holy Spirit. The first miracle of the Holy Spirit was Pentecost when the disciples were filled with the power of the Holy Spirit and began to speak in tongues.

Remember
Some Christians have argued that it does not matter whether the miracles of the New Testament really happened or not. What is important is the spiritual message about God's love for humanity which lies behind these miracles.

Key texts
Acts 1:1–11 – Jesus' ascension into heaven
Acts 2:1–11 – the coming of the Holy Spirit at Pentecost

2.1 Private worship

For many Christians worship is one of the most important ways of expressing belief and is centred on their local Christian community, which in turn is part of a worldwide community of Christians. This is called the Church. Many Christians also worship on their own in private or with their family at home. They may choose readings from the Bible and then pray to worship God.

Rudolf Otto (1869–1937) said that when people experience a sense of awe it is a feeling that reminds us of our own smallness. He used the word 'numinous' (the presence of God which inspires awe and reverence) and called this feeling the 'wholly other'. It is this sense of the 'wholly other' which many feel when they worship.

Main facts

Types of private worship:

- Some people pray, and want to spend time talking to God.
- Some people meditate, they sit quietly, try to empty their minds of ordinary thought and, they would say, listen to their spiritual feelings.
- Some belong to house groups which are small local groups that meet locally for friendship, Bible study and prayer.
- Some people read the Bible with the help of a study book to enable them to better understand the Bible and their faith.

Key person

Rudolf Otto (1869–1937) – a Christian theologian who wrote about the idea of the numinous

Key words

Awe: a feeling of amazement and respect.
Meditate: to empty the mind of thoughts, or concentrate on one thing, in order to aid spiritual thoughts.
Numinous: a mysterious power that suggests the presence of a spirit or god.
Prayer: talking to God.
Wonder: amazement at something.

Remember

Not all Christians worship in the same way – there are as many different types of worship as there are Christians.

2.2 Public worship

The Eucharist is a form of worship common to most Christians, but many Christians also attend other services of worship. This usually consists of prayers, Bible readings, hymns and a sermon. These services stress the importance of the Word and of hearing the teachings of the Bible and of worshipping and praying to God.

Main facts

- Most Christians attend religious services to worship God with others.
- The Eucharist (from a Greek word meaning 'thanksgiving') is common to most Christians and even those who generally worship with a service of the Word will generally celebrate it from time to time. This service celebrates the Last Supper which Jesus ate with his disciples.
- For many Christians, the celebration of the Eucharist and receiving Holy Communion is at the centre of their worship: it is a sacrament, which means that it is a special way of receiving grace.
- Another form of Christian worship is called charismatic and can be found across all Christian denominations. Here people try to open themselves to the Holy Spirit and be inspired by it. Charismatic worship often includes 'glossolalia' or speaking in tongues which is also found in the Acts of the Apostles.
- Worship may also include actions such as charity work, pilgrimages or singing, praising and thanking God.

Key people

Jesus and the disciples – celebrating the Last Supper

Remember

There are many different names for the Eucharist including: Mass, Liturgy, Holy Communion, Lord's Supper, Breaking of Bread, etc. Also the Eucharist is celebrated in many different ways.

Key words

Eucharist: a Christian sacrament that commemorates the Last Supper, with the priest or minister consecrating bread and wine that is consumed by the congregation.
Glossolalia: speaking in tongues.
Liturgy: (1) a formal arrangement of worship; (2) name for the Eucharist in the Orthodox Church.
Sacrament: an outward, physical sign of an inward, invisible grace.
Service: organised worship.
Service of the Word: a church service, or part of one, consisting of Bible readings and preaching.

Key texts

Acts 2:1–11 – the coming of the Holy Spirit at Pentecost
1 Corinthians 11:23b–25 – St Paul's account of the Last Supper

2.3 Prayer and meditation

Prayer is an expression of a Christian's relationship with and dependence on God. It is a conversation with God. In prayer believers may offer praise, make a request of God, or simply express their thoughts and emotions. Prayer should also be a time for listening to God.

Main facts

- There are four main types of prayer and the easiest way to remember them is by using the letters A.C.T.S:
  - A = Adoration
  - C = Confession
  - T = Thanksgiving
  - S = Supplication.
- One of the commonest forms of prayer, particularly in the Roman Catholic Church, is the use of the rosary. The rosary consists of a string of beads with a crucifix. The beads are divided into five sets of one large bead and ten smaller ones. Each set of ten beads is called a decade. During the recitation of the rosary people reflect on one of the four sets of mysteries:
  - Joyful Mysteries
  - Sorrowful Mysteries
  - Glorious Mysteries
  - Luminous Mysteries.

  Each of these sets is based on events in the life of Jesus and the Virgin Mary. The names are general descriptions of the type of events. At the same time they say prayers:
  - Our Father
  - Glory Be
  - Hail Mary
  - Hail, Holy Queen
  - the Apostles' Creed.
- Sometimes Christians may meditate; they sit quietly and try to empty their minds of ordinary thought and listen to their spiritual feelings.

Remember

Prayer is a two-way spiritual relationship in which the Christian should not only talk to God but also listen to what God might be saying to them.

Key words

Adoration: worshipping God for who he is and what he has.
Confession: people saying sorry for things that they have done wrong and asking God's forgiveness.
Meditation: emptying the mind of thoughts to aid spiritual development.
Rosary: a set of beads and prayers used in worship.
Spiritual: religious things rather than worldly ones.
Supplication: prayers in which people ask God for their own needs and those of others.
Thanksgiving: a prayer or act which gives thanks to God.

Key texts

Lord's Prayer – the prayer which Jesus taught his disciples (Matthew 6:9b–13)
Hail Mary – a prayer which praises the Virgin Mary and asks for her help

2.4 Art and music in worship

The majority of Christian denominations use both art and music in their worship. However, others such as the Religious Society of Friends (Quakers) do not use either. They believe that true worship of God is found by sitting in silence until the Holy Spirit moves one of them to speak.

Main facts

- There are different ways in which belief in God can be expressed: in art; in religious buildings; in music; and in the religious ceremonies in which people worship.
- From the very earliest times mosaics showing Christ in majesty in heaven, such as the one in Ravenna, Italy, were used in churches.
- For centuries, when the Bible was not read in a language that most people could understand, its message was conveyed largely by visual means. Stained glass windows were one of the most popular ways in the UK.
- In Orthodox churches there are usually many icons (pictures) of the saints and Jesus. These are seen as a bridge between a person and a religious figure. Worshippers say that an icon seeks to evoke an experience of stillness. The gaze of the icon seems directed at the viewer in an intimate and personal way.
- Some churches, particularly Roman Catholic ones, will have the Stations of the Cross around the walls. These may be pictures or plaques and each one recalls an event in the last days of Jesus' life.
- From the earliest days of Christian worship, believers have sung hymns of praise and thanksgiving to God and used music to express their feelings.
- The main strands in Christian music are communal praise expressed largely in hymns, music for reflection and music for specific occasions.
- Pentecostal worship may include songs sung using a whiteboard or screen and accompanied by guitars and other modern instruments.
- Gospel music has also become very popular as a way of expressing belief.

Key words

Hymn: a song of praise to God.
Icon: a holy picture of Jesus Christ, the Virgin Mary or a saint, usually an oil painting on a wooden panel, found mainly in Orthodox churches.
Mosaic: a picture made with small pieces of coloured material.
Stained glass windows: originally used in churches as a way of telling Bible stories.
Stations of the Cross: a series of fourteen pictures or plaques found around the walls of some churches which recall events in the last days of Jesus' life.

Remember

The place of art in Christian life and worship is very important. Except for some Protestant churches, most Christians use pictures or statues, in particular of Jesus on the cross, to convey messages about their beliefs.

Key text

Exodus 20:4–6 – 'do not make graven images'

2.5 Symbolism in worship

In the early centuries of Christianity, it was often difficult and dangerous for Christians to keep in touch with one another, so they used symbols. These reminded them of important beliefs and could be very encouraging for people who were being persecuted. Symbols can also be clothes, food, actions or gestures as well as pictures.

Main facts

Some of the most common Christian symbols are:

- Alpha and omega – the first and last letters of the Greek alphabet, meaning that Jesus is the beginning and the end of all things.
- A fish – the initial letters from the Greek phrase meaning 'Jesus Christ, Son of God, Saviour' make up the Greek word for fish ('icthus').
- A dove – symbol of peace, or the Holy Spirit.
- Chi-rho – the first two letters of Jesus' name in Greek.
- The cross – the most common Christian symbol.
- The crucifix – a cross with the figure of Jesus on it.
- Candles – to represent Jesus as the Light of the World.

Key words

Alpha: the first letter of the Greek alphabet.
Chi-rho: the first two letters of Jesus' name in Greek.
Crucifix: a cross with the figure of Jesus on it.
Icthus: 'fish' in Greek. Used for the name of Jesus.
Omega: the last letter of the Greek alphabet.
Symbol: a way of explaining the unexplainable, and using something to represent something else.

Remember

Battles have been fought over the question of whether churches should be decorated and should use symbols or not: some people see the church building as reflecting the glory of God, while others say it should reflect the simplicity of Jesus' message. Other Christians believe that pictures or statues are graven images which are forbidden by the second commandment.

2.6 Food and fasting

Christianity does not have strict rules about food and fasting. Christians may eat any sort of food, and although some Christians may choose to be vegetarian there is no rule about this.

Main facts

- Some Christians eat certain foods at certain times, for example some people will follow the old tradition of not eating meat on a Friday (often fish was substituted) in memory of Jesus' crucifixion.
- Traditional foods are eaten at certain festivals:
  - hot-cross buns on Good Friday
  - pancakes on Shrove Tuesday
  - mince pies are traditionally eaten at Christmas, because of the richness of their ingredients at a time of celebration but they have no direct religious connection.
- Some food is symbolic, such as eggs at Easter which symbolise new life.
- Many Christians celebrate Harvest Festival in the autumn when God is thanked for the successful gathering in of the harvest. People take produce to the church and this is afterwards given to the poor.
- Fasting is usually when people go without food or drink for a period of time. For Christians there were two main periods of fasting: Lent, which is the time of preparation for Easter, and Advent, which is the time of preparation for Christmas. Today people no longer fast during Advent, but Lent is still observed. Some people give up luxuries for Lent while others may take something up such as more regular prayer, charity work or going to Lenten classes.
- In the past it was usual for Roman Catholics to fast for twelve hours before receiving communion. Now this has been reduced to just one hour.

Remember

Many Christian churches have special collections for countries in the world that do not have a plentiful food supply and collect money to support aid agencies such as the Catholic Agency for Overseas Development (CAFOD) and Christian Aid.

Key words

Christmas: the celebration of Jesus' birth.
Easter: the celebration of Jesus rising from the dead.
Fasting: abstaining from food for a religious reason.
Lent: the period of forty days which leads up to Easter and recalls the forty days when Jesus fasted in the wilderness.

Key text

Luke 4:1–2 – Jesus' temptation in the desert

3.1 Body and Soul

According to the Bible, God created humans in his own image. Many Christians believe that it is the soul which makes humans like God.

Main facts

- The soul is described as the non-physical part of a person while the body is the physical part.
- Christianity teaches that all humans have an immortal soul. This means that it is a part of them which does not die when their physical body dies, but lives on and goes with them to heaven.
- Christians believe that the soul is the 'breath of life' which God gave to Adam.
- Christianity teaches that when Eve picked the fruit from the Tree of the Knowledge of Good and Evil in the Garden of Eden, she introduced 'original sin' into the world.
- Original sin is the way in which humans are born with a lack of holiness about them, and this is different from any actual sins that people commit themselves.
- Original sin is cleansed when someone is baptised.
- Christian teaching about the importance of the crucifixion of Jesus is that Jesus, as part of the Trinity, was the Son of God, God in human form.
- When Jesus died and was resurrected three days later he atoned for the 'original sin' of Adam and Eve and overcame the power of death.
- In this way humans were forgiven their sins because Jesus' death, which he chose willingly, cleansed humanity which meant that people's immortal souls were now able to survive death and reach heaven.

Key people

Adam and Eve – the first man and woman who introduced original sin into the world

Jesus – atoned for the sins of humanity by his death

St Francis of Assisi (1181–1226) – a Christian saint who gained a reputation of being the friend of animals

Remember

For Christianity, it is the soul which separates humans from animals. Most Christians do not believe that animals have souls as it was only to Adam that God gave the breath of life. However, some people, such as St Francis of Assisi, disagreed with this view.

Key words

Atonement: the Christian belief that the death of Jesus Christ brought about a reconciliation between God and humanity. Jesus was the Saviour or Redeemer of the world.

Baptism: a Christian ceremony of purification with water.

Immortal: having eternal life.

Original sin: the sin which Eve brought into the world when she picked the fruit from the Tree of the Knowledge of Good and Evil in the Garden of Eden.

Soul: that part of a person which is separate from their physical body.

Trinity: Christians believe that God has three persons: God the Father, God the Son and God the Holy Spirit.

Key texts

Genesis 1:26–27 – God made humans in his own image

Genesis 2:7 – God gives Adam the 'breath of life'

Genesis 3:6–12, 16–19 – Adam and Eve eat the fruit from the Tree of the Knowledge of Good and Evil in the Garden of Eden

1 Corinthians 15:22, 42b–44 – physical bodies and spiritual bodies, saved through Jesus

3.2 Life after death

Christians believe that because of Jesus' crucifixion they are freed from the punishment of original sin and now have the chance to go to heaven depending on the way in which they live their lives.

Main facts

- Christian teaching is that one day Jesus will return to earth. This event is called the 'Parousia' or 'second coming'. At this time God will judge everyone.
- Some Christians believe that this judgement takes place as soon as someone dies, while others believe that there will be a Day of Judgement in the future.
- Christians believe those who have ignored the teachings of Jesus and the Bible will be sent to hell where they will receive eternal punishment.
- Christians believe those who have accepted Jesus as their saviour and followed his teachings will go to heaven.
- The Roman Catholic Church teaches that there is also another place called purgatory. People who have been good Christians but have still committed some sins go to purgatory where they are fully cleansed until they are in a state ready for heaven. Purgatory is not a place of judgement and people go from purgatory to heaven but never from purgatory to hell.

Key person

Jesus – Christians believe that one day he will return to earth

Remember

Christians do not believe in reincarnation. Christianity teaches that people have 'one soul and one life to save it in'.

Key text

1 Corinthians 15:51–52 – teaching about the Day of Judgement

Key words

Crucifixion: when Jesus was crucified on the cross in Jerusalem.
Heaven: where Christians hope to go after death in the sight of God.
Hell: where wicked people may go after death, denied the sight of God.
Judgement: when God judges people according to how they have lived their lives.
Parousia: (second coming) the anticipated and prophesied return of Jesus Christ to judge humanity at the end of the world.
Purgatory: Roman Catholic belief that after death many souls go to purgatory where they are prepared to go to heaven.
Sin: an action which goes against religious teachings.

3.3 Beliefs about heaven

Christian belief is that death is not something which people should be frightened of but that they should look forward to a life in heaven when there will be no more suffering and where they will live happily with God for ever.

Main facts

- Views of heaven have changed over the centuries since the beginning of Christianity. In the medieval world heaven was described as a magical place with angels sitting on clouds and playing harps.
- These views were probably based on teachings found in the Old Testament such as Ezekiel's vision of the throne of God.
- Another view of heaven can be found in the book of Revelation in the New Testament with the idea that there will be no more suffering and God will rule the earth.
- One of the ideas about heaven is that when people arrive there they will see the 'Beatific Vision': this is an eternal and direct view of God which gives people total happiness.
- Some Christians believe that the statement in the Apostles' Creed means that when people get to heaven they will be in their physical bodies: 'I believe … in the resurrection of the body'.
- Many Christians believe that heaven is something like a state of mind and is not a physical thing which can be described.

Remember

Most non-believers are not afraid of death in the way in which some believers are. For people with a religious belief there can be a fear that, however hard they may try, they will not be judged good enough to go to heaven after death. If someone does not believe in any afterlife then this fear is removed.

Key words

Beatific vision: the sight of God.
Resurrection: the body will come back to life after death.

Key texts

Ezekiel 1:25–28 – the vision of God's throne
Revelation 4:1–8 – God's throne in Heaven
Apostles' Creed – 'I believe in the resurrection of the body'

3.4 Beliefs about hell and purgatory

Christian teaching about heaven, hell and purgatory varies between denominations but very few Christians still believe that these are physical places, such as the idea that hell has everlasting fires to torture people.

Main facts

- Original Christian teaching is that people who did not accept Jesus as their saviour and follow his teachings would be sent to hell after death and would be punished there for eternity.
- Hell was described as a place of torture, with everlasting fires burning, although many Christians no longer believe this.
- Most Christians today would probably say that hell is a state of mind or that it is the denial of the Beatific Vision.
- Christian teaching has always been that if people have had the opportunity to hear about Jesus and then chosen not to accept and follow him, they cannot enter heaven.
- However, the Roman Catholic Church teaches that heaven is not necessarily closed to those who have never encountered Christianity: 'Those who, through no fault of their own, do not know the Gospel of Christ or his Church, but who nevertheless seek God with a sincere heart, and, moved by grace, try in their actions to do his will as they know it through the dictates of their conscience – those too may achieve eternal salvation' (*Ad gentes* [To the Nations] 7).
- The Roman Catholic Church teaches that very few people are ready to go to heaven when they die. Although they have lived good Christian lives they are still not free from sin.
- When they die these people go to purgatory rather than to heaven. They stay here until their souls are ready for heaven. People who go to purgatory will reach heaven eventually and are not at risk of going to hell.
- '... the faithful who are still pilgrims on earth are able to help the souls in purgatory by offering prayers in suffrage for them, especially the Eucharistic sacrifice. They also help them by almsgiving, indulgences, and works of penance' (Catechism of the Catholic Church 211).

Remember

Purgatory is a belief of Roman Catholic Christians but many other Christians do not believe in it as there is nothing in the Bible about it.

Key texts

Matthew 25:31–46 – the Parable of the Sheep and the Goats
Luke 16:19–31 – the Parable of the Rich Man and Lazarus

Key words

Penance: an act to show regret for having sinned.
Saviour: someone who rescues someone else.

3.5 Salvation, redemption and the suffering of Christ, and judgement

Christianity teaches that through Jesus' suffering humanity received redemption for the original sin. This redemption has allowed humans the possibility of reaching heaven. In order to reach heaven Christianity teaches that after death God will judge people for the way in which they have lived their lives. Christians believe it is important to show care for others and to show devotion to Jesus.

Main facts

- There are two kinds of judgement in Christian teaching:
  - 'General' Judgement or the Last Judgement when God will pass his final sentence on the whole of humanity as well as on the soul and body of each individual.
  - 'Particular' Judgement is the judgement given to every soul when a person dies.
- Humans were forgiven their sins because Jesus' death, which he chose willingly, cleansed humanity which meant that people's immortal souls were now able to survive death and reach heaven. In this way people achieved redemption.
- Christians believe they will be judged on the concern they show to others. Jesus' teaching in the Parable of the Sheep and the Goats shows that people who care for others will receive eternal life, but people who simply ignore the suffering of others will be punished in hell.
- Christians believe that they will receive salvation and redemption through devotion to Jesus. This teaching can be found in Paul's Epistle to the Romans.
- Roman Catholics, and some Anglicans, believe that people can help themselves lead better lives by confessing their sins to a priest who will forgive them.

Remember

The crucifixion and resurrection of Jesus is central to all Christian beliefs about salvation, redemption and judgement.

Key texts

Matthew 16:18–19 – Jesus promises Peter the keys of heaven
Matthew 25:31–46 – the Parable of the Sheep and the Goats
Luke 16:19–31 – the Parable of the Rich Man and Lazarus
Luke 23:40–43 – Jesus speaks to the criminals while he is on the cross
John 20:23 – forgiveness of sins
Romans 8:1–3a – Paul explains that Jesus was sent to save people
Revelation 21:1–2, 4b – a new Jerusalem

Key words

Redemption: Jesus saved people from punishment for the sins of humanity and redeemed them.
Salvation: Jesus saved people from the consequences of sin.

3.6 Funeral rites

Funeral services are an opportunity for the relatives and friends of the dead person to show their respect and say a final 'goodbye' to them. Christian funeral services are based on the teachings of the Bible and contain words and symbols which are chosen to comfort the relatives and express Christian beliefs.

Main facts

- When a Christian is dying a Christian minister will try to visit them to help them prepare for their death. The person may wish to confess their sins to the minister and, for Roman Catholics, they may wish to receive a sacrament which is known as the Anointing of the Sick.
- The person is anointed with the Oil of Unction, which is consecrated every year by a bishop at the Chrism Mass on Holy (Maundy) Thursday.
- Christian funeral services usually take place in a church and the body is then either buried or cremated.
- The opening of a funeral service is usually the reading of this passage from John: 'I am the resurrection and the life. He who believes in me will live, even though he dies; and whoever lives and believes in me will never die' (John 11:25b–26a).
- At the service some Christians may have a Requiem Mass.
- Churches are often decorated with white flowers to represent the new life with God which the person is now entering.
- As the body is finally laid to rest the priest or minister will say, 'ashes to ashes, dust to dust', based on Genesis 3:19.
- Candles are lit as a reminder that Christians are saved because Jesus was the 'Light of the World'. Also the rising smoke is sometimes said to represent the soul or prayers for the soul rising to heaven.
- A gravestone is placed at the site later. This contains details of the person's life and often a prayer or quotation from the Bible. Relatives and friends may put flowers on the grave particularly at Christmas and Easter and on the date of the dead person's birthday. These are both ways in which people reinforce their beliefs that the person is now with God but is not forgotten.

Remember

Although black is a traditional colour for mourning, Christians do not see funerals as sad events as they celebrate the new life with God which the dead person is now entering.

Key words

Anointing of the Sick: a sacrament given to those who are sick or dying.
Chrism Mass: a special mass on Holy (Maundy) Thursday at which oils are consecrated.
Maundy Thursday: the day on which Jesus ate the Last Supper with his disciples.
Oil of Unction: the oil used in the Anointing of the Sick.
Requiem Mass: a special mass said at a funeral.

Key texts

Genesis 3:19 – you will return to dust
John 8:12 – Jesus as the light of the world
John 11:25b–26a – 'I am the resurrection and the life'
James 5:14–15 – anointing of the sick

4.1 Concepts of good and evil: God and the Devil (Satan)

Christianity teaches that God is much more powerful than the Devil and that therefore good is much stronger than evil. However, it also says that God created people with free will so that they could decide what to do for themselves. This means that people are free to choose bad over good even though they know the probable consequences of their actions.

Main facts

- For Christians, God is the beginning of everything and everything which God created is good.
- Some Christians say that if there is evil in the world then there must also be a power of evil as well as a power of good. This power is often referred to as the Devil.
- Some people would say that there is no such thing as the Devil and that it is just people who chose to be evil. For example: they might say that Blessed Mother Teresa chose to be good and Saddam Hussein chose to be evil.
- The story of the origins of the Devil as a fallen angel is not found in the Bible but in other religious books called the Apocrypha, which were not thought suitable to include in the Bible itself.
- There are very few references to Satan in the Bible, although he does appear at the beginning of Jesus' ministry when he tempts him in the wilderness for forty days.

Key words

Apocrypha: Jewish and Christian religious writings which are not included in the Bible.
Good and evil: God is seen as being totally good while the Devil is totally evil.

Remember

Sometimes people use the words 'good' and 'evil' without really thinking what they mean by them. The question is, how do people make these judgements about what is 'right' and 'wrong' or 'good' and 'evil'? They might say that they just 'know' but for philosophers the question needs more consideration.

Key texts

Genesis 1:31a – everything that God made was good
Luke 4:1–13 – Jesus' temptation in the wilderness
Luke 10:18 – reference to the Devil
Revelation 12:7–9, 17 – reference to the Devil

4.2 The Fall, original sin and redemption

By rising from the dead, Jesus 'atoned' for the 'original sin' of humanity and overcame the power of death. People were redeemed from their sins because he died.

Main facts

- According to the Bible, Eve picked the fruit from the Tree of the Knowledge of Good and Evil in the Garden of Eden when this had been forbidden by God.
- When she did this Eve introduced 'original sin' into the world.
- This event is called the Fall and was when Adam and Eve were driven out of the Garden of Eden.
- According to the teaching of the Roman Catholic Church, original sin is the way in which humans are born with a lack of holiness about them, and this is different from any actual sins that people commit themselves.
- Some Christians believe that being made in the image of God, humans would have been immortal, but that they lost their immortality when they ate the fruit.
- The actual phrase 'original sin' does not appear in the Bible but the idea is found in Paul's letter to the Romans.
- In the first letter to the Corinthians, Paul explains the importance of the crucifixion of Jesus. Jesus was the Son of God and allowed himself to be crucified by the Romans. He died and three days later came back from the dead in order to defeat death and sin and so reopen the way to God.

Key words

The Fall: when Adam and Eve ate the forbidden fruit.
Original sin: the sin which Eve brought into the world when she picked the fruit from the Tree of the Knowledge of Good and Evil in the Garden of Eden.
Redemption: by dying on the cross, Jesus saved humanity from the consequences of original sin.

Key people

Adam and Eve – first man and woman who brought original sin into the world
Jesus – saved humanity from the consequences of sin
Paul – one of the letter writers of the early Church

Remember

In Christianity today, original sin is washed away by the sacrament of baptism when a baby or adult is first welcomed into the Church. After this, in Roman Catholic Christianity, people can receive absolution from their sins by making their confession to a priest.

Key texts

Romans 5:12 – how sin entered the world
1 Corinthians 15:22 – how Jesus saved humanity from the consequences of sin

4.3 What is the problem of evil?

It is an undeniable fact that there is evil in the world and this inevitably causes problems for Christians. If God is omnipotent (all-powerful), omniscient (all-knowing) and omnibenevolent (all-good), how can God allow evil to exist?

Main facts

Christians say that there are two kinds of evil:

- Moral evil: the deeds or behaviour of people which are seen to be cruel and uncaring. The twentieth-century Holocaust might be described as moral evil.
- Natural evil: this covers natural events such as volcanoes, floods and hurricanes, which may harm or kill people but do not appear to be caused by human beings. An example of this could be the 2004 Boxing Day Asian tsunami.

Some people argue that some of the events which are described as natural evil are caused indirectly by humans because they could be the effect of climate change and environmental destruction. Some Christians also believe that natural evil is caused by the Devil.

However, many of the people who are the victims of these events lived good lives so the question remains as to why God would allow them to suffer in this way.

Key person

Adolf Hitler (1889–1945) – German leader responsible for the Holocaust during the Second World War

Key words

Climate change: weather effects produced by man-made means.
Holocaust: the murder of six million Jews during the Second World War (1939–45).
Moral evil: the acts of people which are seen to be cruel and uncaring.
Natural evil: natural disasters such as hurricanes.
Omnibenevolent: all-good.
Omnipotent: all-important.
Omniscient: all-present.
Tsunami: a large destructive ocean wave.

Remember

Some people might argue that a good God would not allow evil and suffering in the world while many Christians would argue that God has a purpose for evil and suffering.

4.4 Responses to the problem of evil

Christians believe that God has a plan which allows evil and suffering in the world, but that this plan is beyond the comprehension of human kind.

Main facts

- Some people might argue that a good God would not allow evil and suffering in the world. If this is the case then there are a number of options:
  - God does not exist
  - God is not all-powerful
  - God is actually responsible for everything so is responsible for evil and suffering as well as good.
- One of the arguments put forward to explain the existence of pain and suffering is that Adam and Eve disobeyed God in the Garden of Eden. Yet why did God allow them to disobey and choose evil if they had been created perfect?
- Irenaeus (130–202) said that people needed to suffer and needed to be made to choose between good and evil, otherwise they would be like obedient automatons or robots and God wants people to choose to worship him. However, how does this apply to the suffering of babies?
- St Augustine (354–430) believed that evil was a lack of good. Evil happens when people do not choose good and to live according to the standards which God has set for human beings. This means that evil is not a thing in itself, but simply what is left when there is no good present.
- In the story of Job in the Old Testament, Job is a good man who worships God and lives a good life. A figure called the 'Adversary' asks God's permission to test Job to see just how devoted he is to God. God is confident of Job's devotion and gives permission. Job loses his wife, his children, his animals, all his wealth and his health but does not lose his faith and finally he is rewarded by God.

Key word

Suffering: physical or mental pain or distress.

Key people

Adam and Eve – the first man and woman who introduced original sin into the world

Adversary – the person who makes Job suffer, sometimes translated as Satan

Job – man who suffered as a test of his faith

Irenaeus (130–202) – Christian saint who said that people needed to suffer otherwise they would be like obedient robots

St Augustine (354–430) – Christian saint who believed that evil was a lack of good

Remember

Non-believers might say that all human beings have the choice of how to behave. They can either choose to live their lives and behave in a way which is good for themselves and for other people, or they can live in a way which might seem good for them but which is damaging for others.

Key texts

Genesis 2–3 – the introduction of original sin into the world

Job – the story of a man whose faith is tested but never gives up hope in God

4.5 Coping with suffering

One way of dealing with problems of evil and suffering is just to say that they are part of God's purpose which cannot be understood by humans.

Main facts

- At the time of the New Testament many people believed that illness and suffering were punishments for sins that people had committed. They also believed they were being punished for the original sin of Adam and Eve.
- Christianity teaches that God took human form and came to earth as Jesus of Nazareth.
- Jesus gave his life by dying on the cross and because he was innocent of any sin and chose to die for others, the sins of humans were forgiven.
- Because of Jesus, Christians believe that God shared in human suffering.
- When they are suffering, many Christians pray to God either alone or as a community to help them or to give them the strength.
- Christians accept that God does not always answer prayers in the way they would like him to, but that God chooses the best for them.
- An example of faith taking away the suffering of sin is found in Matthew's gospel when Jesus heals a paralytic: 'Take heart, son; your sins are forgiven.'

Key people

Adam and Eve – the first man and woman who introduced original sin into the world
Jesus – healed people with miracles
Paralytic – man healed by Jesus

Remember

Christians believe that God answers their prayers, but not always in the way that they hoped.

Key words

Illness: disease or sickness.
Paralytic: someone suffering from paralysis.
Prayer: an address to God.
Sin: behaviour which goes against religious teaching.
Suffering: physical or mental pain or distress.

Key text

Matthew 9:1–8 – Jesus heals a paralytic

4.6 Sources and reasons for moral behaviour

For Christians there are three main sources and reasons for moral behaviour: the Bible, faith in Christ and conscience. Roman Catholics would also consider the teaching of the Church and the Pope as a source of authority for moral behaviour.

Main facts

- Christianity teaches that because Jesus gave up his life willingly and was innocent of any sin, his death atoned for all the sins of humanity so that all those who have followed his teachings and accepted him as the Son of God now have the opportunity to reach heaven when they die.
- As well as following the Ten Commandments and Jesus' teaching in the Sermon on the Mount, Christians also follow the two Great Commandments:
  - 'Hear, O Israel, the Lord our God, the Lord is one. Love the Lord your God with all your heart and with all your soul and with all your mind and with all your strength.'
  - 'Love your neighbour as yourself.'
  Christians also follow the Golden Rule:
  - 'So in everything, do to others what you would have them do to you, for this sums up the Law and the Prophets.'
- Another way in which Christians might decide how God wants them to behave is by following the example of Jesus' life and teachings as found in the New Testament. Because Christians have faith in Jesus as their saviour and the Son of God the example of his life is a model for Christians to follow.
- People often say that they 'know' what to do because they are following their conscience. Sometimes people may feel that they cannot do something because their conscience will not allow it.
- It is difficult to say what this 'conscience' is. Many Christians would say that it is the 'voice of God' telling them what to do.

Remember

Most of the ways in which Christians find teachings and help in deciding about moral behaviour are not relevant to non-believers. However, many Humanists, for example, do believe in a conscience but they do not think that this comes from God.

Key words

Bible: the sacred text of Christianity.
Commandments: laws.
Conscience: a sense of what is right and wrong.
Faith: belief or trust in something without proof.

Key texts

Exodus 20:1–17 – the Ten Commandments
Matthew 5–7 – the Sermon on the Mount
Mark 12:28–31 – the two Great Commandments

5.1 Concept of revelation

Revelation means 'unveiling' – something which was previously hidden becomes known and for Christians this comes from God.

Main facts

- Christians believe that God can reveal himself directly to them. Many Christians have had personal experience of God when they feel he speaks directly to them. This may be through prayer, when on a pilgrimage, when meditating on a passage from the Bible, or when they simply feel awe in the presence of God or feel loved by God.
- There are two types of revelation – general (or natural) revelation and special revelation:
  - General or natural revelation: this is called general because it is made available to everyone, and is natural because it comes to us through nature. This type of revelation is found in the beauty and complexity of the natural world. William Paley (1743–1805) saw the design of the natural world as evidence for the existence of God as its designer. Christians also see the conscience as part of this revelation.
  - Special revelation is what God has taken the initiative to give, such as is told in the Bible. For example, in the Old Testament there are accounts of God acting in special ways, such as leading the Israelites through the desert, and through special people such as the prophets, speaking and gradually making his character and plans known. Some Christians would say that the Bible is the Word of God and that it is all that they need because it tells people exactly what God is like and what he wants. Roman Catholics, in particular, would regard the teachings of the Church as part of this special revelation.

Key words

Conscience: a sense of right and wrong.
Revelation: 'unveiling' – when something which was previously hidden becomes known.

Key person

William Paley (1743–1805) – a clergyman who saw the design of the natural world as evidence for the existence of God

Remember

People can never really know each other, or what other people are thinking about. However, people can know us and what we are thinking if we tell them. Christians believe that it is exactly the same with God's revelation.

Key texts

Psalm 19:1–4 – God is revealed through the world
John 1:14, 18 – Jesus as the Word of God
Romans 1:19–20 – God shows himself through creation
2 Timothy 3:16 – 'All Scripture is God-breathed'
Hebrews 1:1–3 – God speaks to the world through Jesus

5.2 Revelation through conversion

Revelation of God can be through the mystical and religious experiences that people experience, such as conversion. For Christians, conversion means becoming a believer.

Main facts

- One form of revelation through religious experience is conversion.
- There are many examples of conversion in the Bible, but one of the most important is the conversion of St Paul after he had been persecuting some of the first Christians.
- Evangelical Christians see conversion as the beginning of faith. A person has to admit their sins to God and ask for his forgiveness. Evangelical Christians call this being 'born again' or 'saved'.
- For some Christians conversion is the most important experience of their lives and changes them forever. They believe that God has revealed himself to them in a very particular way.
- Sometimes Christians have actual physical experiences like Paul when they are converted and people who are sick may be healed.
- Conversion can happen in all Christian denominations through conversations with others, through Bible reading or through prayer.

Key words

Conversion: a change in someone's religious beliefs.
Evangelical Christians: Protestant Christians who emphasise the authority of the Bible and salvation through the personal acceptance of Jesus Christ.
Experience: something which happens to somebody.
Forgiveness: pardoning someone for a mistake or wrongful act.

Key person

Saul/Paul – a Jew who was converted by Jesus on the road to Damascus

Remember

Non-believers might think that people who have a conversion experience are experiencing some sort of psychological experience rather than a direct revelation from God.

Key text

Acts 9:1–19a – the conversion of Paul

5.3 Revelation through other mystical and religious experiences

Most Christians believe that God reveals himself to them, and speaks directly to them.

Main facts

- Some Christians, after their conversion, have a later experience of 'baptism in the spirit'. The Holy Spirit is said to touch them in a particular way and they are given spiritual gifts such as speaking in tongues (glossolalia), prophesying, or having visions. These spiritual gifts started on the first day of Pentecost when the Holy Spirit came to the disciples.
- Some worshippers will feel very close to God and worship in an uninhibited way: singing, dancing, clapping and holding their hands in the air. This is called charismatic worship. In the second half of the twentieth century the Charismatic Movement spread to mainstream churches. Many Christians believe that the spiritual gifts are a form of revelation by which God communicates directly with people.
- Prayer and meditation are the ways in which many Christians believe God reveals himself to them.
- Meditation or contemplative prayer for Christians is not just emptying their mind but filling it with God's word. It may involve a single word or prayer such as the Jesus Prayer. It has been described as listening for God; opening yourself to God; waiting silently upon God. It is also called 'the prayer of quiet'.

Key words

Baptism: a Christian ceremony when someone is cleansed of original sin.
Charismatic: form of Christian worship where people try to open themselves to the Holy Spirit and be inspired by it.
Glossolalia: speaking in tongues.
Holy Spirit: the third person of the Trinity.
Pentecost: the day when the Holy Spirit came to the disciples.
Prophesying: predicting future events.

Key person

Paul – one of the letter writers of the early Church

Remember

From the very beginning of the Christian Church the gifts of the Spirit have caused some difficulties when they have not been thought of as genuine. Paul explained that people may receive different gifts but that they all come from the Spirit and should be used to help others.

Key texts

Acts 2:1–11 – the coming of the Holy Spirit at Pentecost
Jesus Prayer – Jesus, Son of God have mercy on me

5.4 Revelation of God in the person of Jesus

Jesus was born as man. Christians believe that God became a human being in the person of Jesus – the incarnation. Jesus, it is believed, was fully human and fully God. 'Incarnation' means literally 'in flesh'.

Main facts

- Paul wrote that God reveals himself through Jesus, in order that people can know God through Jesus' life, his work and his teachings.
- Christians believe that Jesus reveals God to humanity because Jesus enters into a relationship with people and creates a relationship between people.
- Christians believe Jesus reveals God's nature through the Gospel stories of how he showed love and forgiveness, offering people a new start in life.
- The Church and Bible teaching is that it was necessary for Jesus to become a human so that he, on behalf of the human race, could make a full atonement for human sin and God's forgiveness was made available to all people.

Key word

Incarnation: God taking human form as Jesus Christ.

Key person

Paul – one of the letter writers of the early Church

Remember

Jesus is referred to as 'The Saviour' and Christians believe that in Jesus Christ they have the fullest revelation of God in a human life.

Key texts

John 14:6b – 'No one comes to the Father except through me'
Colossians 1:15–20 – Jesus is God

5.5 The authority of the Bible

Christians believe the Bible reveals the truth about God; some say it is totally true, others interpret it differently. However, for all Christians it is a central source of authority and is used in public worship, private study, meditation and decision-making.

Main facts

- The Old Testament of the Bible contains the same books as the Jewish Scriptures (the Tenakh), but in a different order. One of the most important ideas in the Old Testament is the relationship between God and humanity.
- The New Testament contains the writings of the early Christians.
- Some Christians will say that every word of the Bible is absolutely true and there are no errors or mistakes in it. These Christians are often called fundamentalists or literalists. Their view is that the Bible is the Word of God and has verbal inerrancy: that means that every word was inspired by God's guidance of the writers through the Holy Spirit and therefore every word is true.
- The view held by Roman Catholics, Orthodox Christians and some Anglicans is that the Holy Spirit, God's gift to the Church, inspired the people who wrote the books.
- The 'conservative' approach to biblical authority, that the authors of the books of the Bible wrote under God's inspiration, is held by many evangelical Protestant Christians.
- The liberal view of the Bible is that it records the experiences of people seriously seeking after God in their own lives, situations and cultures. The words are therefore a product of people trying to understand God and could be seen as a symbolic way of showing God's truth.

Key words

Conservative: belief that the authors of the books of the Bible wrote under God's inspiration.

Fundamentalists: Christians who say that every word of the Bible is absolutely true and there are no errors or mistakes in it.

Liberal: a belief that the Bible need not be understood literally but can be interpreted.

Literalists: See fundamentalists.

New Testament: the second part of the Christian Bible containing the Gospels, the Acts of the Apostles, the Epistles and the book of Revelation.

Old Testament: the first part of the Christian Bible, originally the Tenakh – Jewish Scriptures.

Remember

For Christians the Bible is the most sacred text and is a source of authority. The teachings in the Bible tell Christians what God wants of them and how he wants them to live.

Key text

2 Timothy 3:16 – 'All Scripture is God-breathed'

5.6 Significance and importance of the Bible

The Bible is the most important and holy book for Christians. They try to understand the message of the Bible and live their lives according to its teachings.

Main facts

- Christians believe that the Bible contains the teachings they need to understand God and follow Jesus.
- The Old Testament was written mostly in Hebrew, with some books in Aramaic, and the New Testament was written in Greek.
- The Bible was not translated into English until the sixteenth century by William Tyndale (1494–1536).
- Christians feel it is vital that everyone should be able to read the Bible in their own language, and some languages have even been written down for the first time so that translators could write the Bible in them.
- In every church service there are readings from the Bible and usually the sermon explores and explains the teachings in the passage that has been read.
- Some Christians read the Bible at home every day, and use it to pray. Other Christians might meet together in Bible study groups to read and study passages from the Bible together.

Key person

William Tyndale
(1494–1536) – a theologian who first translated the Bible into English

Key words

Aramaic: a language spoken in the Holy Land at the time of Jesus.
Authority: source of reliable knowledge and teachings.
Greek: the language in which most of the New Testament was originally written.
Sermon: a talk on a religious subject at a service.
Tradition: the teachings of the Church.
Translation: putting a text into another language.

Remember

Most Christians accept the Bible as a source of authority, but some would also accept the teachings and traditions of the Church as another source of authority. In particular Roman Catholics may refer to Church Encyclicals which are formal statements made by the Pope.

6.1 Scientific theories about the origins of the world and humanity

Cosmology and evolution are the two sciences that have proposed theories of the origins of the world and of humanity. Cosmology is about the origins of the universe which most scientists believe was caused by the Big Bang. Evolution is about the development of life forms which most scientists believe came about through a process of natural selection.

Main facts

- The Big Bang theory suggests that a massive explosion led to the creation of the whole universe. The gases and matter released by the explosion formed the stars and planets of the universe.
- Ideas about evolution began in 1740 when Charles Bonnet wrote a paper about aphids and 'preformationism'.
- The founder of evolutionary theory is generally considered to be Charles Darwin who suggested that life began with a simple single cell and evolved and developed through a process of natural selection.
- Many people refused to believe that humans evolved from apes and challenged the theory of evolution because they said it disagreed with the Bible. For example, in the nineteenth century a famous geologist, Philip Gosse, argued that God had placed fossils in rocks to test the faith of Christians. People who still take this view about the theory of evolution are called 'Creationists'.
- Intelligent design is a relatively new theory which is designed to be an alternative to these scientific views. It claims that the universe and its life forms are too complex to have evolved without God. There is no scientific evidence to support this.

Key people

Charles Bonnet (1720–93) – a Swiss naturalist who devised the theory of 'preformationism'
Charles Darwin (1809–82) – developed the theory of natural selection
Philip Gosse (1810–88) – argued that God had placed fossils in rocks to test the faith of Christians

Remember

Being a scientist does not mean that a person is an atheist. There are many scientists who are Christian. Many would argue that not accepting the creation stories does not mean that you cannot believe in God. They believe that God did create everything but that science has now explained how that happened in a way which is obviously more sophisticated than the creation accounts.

Key words

Big Bang theory: scientific theory which suggests that there was a massive explosion about 18 billion years ago and that this led to the creation of the whole universe.
Cosmology: theories about the origins of the universe.
Creationists: people who believe that God created the world in six days as in the biblical accounts.
Evolution: the idea that plants and animals have developed or evolved over time.
Intelligent design: a theory which says that life is so complex that it must have been designed by a higher intelligent being, and did not evolve by natural selection.
Natural selection: theory that tiny differences and genetic mutations between creatures of the same species can sometimes make one individual slightly better suited to their environment than others. This means that it survives longer and has more offspring who inherit that trait.

Key texts

On the Origin of Species by Means of Natural Selection or the Preservation of Favoured Races in the Struggle for Life – Charles Darwin's 1859 book in which he developed the theory of natural selection
Genesis 1–2 – the two Genesis creation stories

6.2 Christian teachings about the origins of the world and humanity

The book of Genesis contains two different accounts of the creation of the world and of humanity. Many scholars believe that the second account is older than the first account.

Main facts

How life and the world came into existence is one of the big questions that have always concerned religious believers. The Christian story of creation and the origins of the world are found in the first book of the Bible, Genesis. Here there are two accounts of creation:

- The first account contains the opening verses of the Bible: 'In the beginning God created the heavens and the earth ... .' The Roman Catholic Church teaches that these verses mean God created the world out of nothing – *ex nihilo*. Some other Christians believe that God created the world out of matter that was already there. So these verses raise the key issue of the problem of evil:
  - If God created the world out of nothing at all and because people believe that God is good, then everything he created would also be good.
  - If God created the world from matter which was already present and there was evil within this matter, this would suggest that God was not necessarily responsible for the existence of evil.
- In this account God creates the world in six days. On day six he creates animals and humans. Human beings are created in his own image and God places them in charge of the whole of creation giving them dominion and stewardship. He tells the humans: 'Be fruitful and increase in number; fill the earth and subdue it.'
- In the second account of creation in Genesis, humans are made before the plants and animals.

Key people

Adam and Eve – the first humans

Remember

The first account of creation shows God making the world in six days. The importance is not how long a day lasted – the Hebrew word 'ayin' simply means a 'period of time', but that it shows that God planned creation and put everything in place and in order.

Key words

Creation: God's making of the universe.
Dominion: power or authority.
Ex nihilo: out of nothing.
Stewardship: looking after something for someone else.

Key texts

Genesis 1–2 – the two Genesis creation stories

6.3 The relationship between scientific and religious understandings of the origins of the world and humanity

The majority of Christians now appear to accept the Big Bang theory of creation even if they also believe that God was present and may have caused the Big Bang.

Main facts

- Problems between scientific and religious accounts of creation are significant for those Christians who believe that the Bible is the exact Word of God, as it is more difficult to reconcile this with scientific discoveries about creation.
- Creationists sometimes support their views with the work of James Ussher, a seventeenth-century English bishop, who calculated the actual time of creation by working through all the dates and times given in the Bible. He eventually worked out that it took place at 9a.m. on 26 October 4004BCE, many billions of years after the date later given by science.
- Many Christians have resolved this difficulty for themselves because they consider the creation accounts to be myths. A myth contains important truths – in this case God is ultimately responsible for the creation of the world and humanity – but it is not supposed to be a factual account of what happened. So scientific and religious understandings can be reconciled: 'Science explains how and religion explains why.'
- In the fourth century, St Augustine said that the biblical accounts did not present a problem to Christianity because God must have invented time when he made the rest of creation. God's creation would have happened outside of time as we understand it.
- Darwin's theory of evolution has also caused a problem for many Christians. It was not finally accepted by the Roman Catholic Church until 1996.
- St Augustine had said that in the beginning God only created germs or causes of the forms of life which were afterwards to be developed. It is possible to put this idea in line with the biblical creation accounts as showing the gradual development of more complex species.

Key people

St Augustine (354–430) – a Christian saint who said that in the beginning God only created germs or causes of the forms of life

James Ussher (1581–1656) – calculated the actual time of creation as being at 9a.m. on 26 October 4004BCE

Charles Darwin (1809–82) – developed the theory of natural selection

Remember

Some people, who do not believe the creation accounts to be myths, say that only one source about creation can be right, either the Bible or science, but not both. Many Christians do not accept this viewpoint.

Key words

Evolution: the scientific theory that all species develop from earlier forms of life.

Myth: a story which attempts to explain the origins of natural phenomena or aspects of human behaviour.

6.4 The place of humanity in relation to animals

Most Christians believe that animals were part of God's creation of the world, even if they are seen as a lesser creation than human beings.

Main facts

- In the creation accounts in Genesis, humans are given power over all the creatures and in Genesis 2 God tells Adam to name the animals. God gave people free choice in the way they treat the world.
- For many centuries there have been discussions among Christians as to whether animals have souls. It appears that when God breathed into Adam he gave humanity something different from the animals.
- It is clear from Jesus' teaching that God cares about animals as well as people: 'Are not five sparrows sold for two pennies? Yet not one of them is forgotten by God' (Luke 12:6).
- St Francis of Assisi (1181–1226) spoke about animals and their treatment. He appears to have believed that animals did have souls.
- There is disagreement among Christians about their attitude towards animals, particularly in relation to their use in scientific research. Some believe that humans were given power over animals and so such research is acceptable, while others feel that animals should be treated with the same care and respect as humans.
- Many Christian Churches have spoken out against the way in which animals are treated. These include the Church of England, the Methodist Church and the Religious Society of Friends (Quakers).
- In 1986, at the World Wide Fund for Nature (WWF), Father Lanfranco Serrini said: 'Every human act of irresponsibility towards creatures is an abomination.'

Key person

St Francis of Assisi (1181–1226) – Christian saint who thought that animals had souls

Remember

In Genesis, people are instructed to act as 'stewards'. 'Be fruitful and increase in number; fill the earth and subdue it. Rule over the fish of the sea and the birds of the air and over every living creature that moves on the ground' (Genesis 1:28b).

'The Lord God took the man and put him in the Garden of Eden to work it and take care of it' (Genesis 2:15). However, stewardship also brings responsibility.

Key word

Soul: the part of a human being which is separate from the physical body.

Key texts

Genesis 2 – Adam names the animals
Luke 12:6 – God cares for the sparrows

6.5 Concept of stewardship and religious teachings relating to environmental issues

The Bible teaches that all life was created by God and Christians see this as making it sacred. Therefore, the world belongs to God, and humans, as his stewards, must care for it.

Main facts

- According to Christianity, at the time of creation people were intended to act as 'stewards' (someone who looks after something for someone else).
- God gave humans dominion – authority and control over creation but not domination.
- The story of Noah in Genesis shows what God requires of humans in caring for the environment. Noah is required to take two of every kind of animal with him in the ark so as to save them from the flood.
- The Nicene Creed emphasises God's role as creator of all life: 'We believe in one God … maker of heaven and earth …'.
- In the Old Testament there are teachings about caring for the land: 'When you lay siege to a city for a long time, fighting against it to capture it, do not destroy its trees by putting an axe to them, because you can eat their fruit. Do not cut them down. Are the trees of the field people, that you should besiege them?' (Deuteronomy 20:19).
- Christianity has always taught that people should only take from the world what they need and that they should not be concerned with material wealth.
- As well as showing great concern towards animals, St Francis of Assisi extended this teaching in relation to the world as a whole.

Key words

Creator: someone who makes or produces something.
Domination: exercising power over a less-powerful being.
Dominion: to have authority or control over something.
Steward: someone who looks after something for someone else.

Key people

Noah – rescued the animals in the ark
St Francis of Assisi (1181–1226) – Christian saint

Remember

In recent years the Churches have become much more concerned about the environment and are often involved in charities and projects to help protect it.

Key texts

Genesis 1–2 – the two Genesis creation stories
Genesis 6:9–8:22 – the story of Noah
Psalm 24 – the glory of God's creation
Luke 12:22–31 – God cares for the birds
Nicene Creed – God is maker of heaven and earth
Canticle of the Sun – St Francis of Assisi's poem about the glory of the created world

6.6 Christian responses to environmental issues

Although humanity has been given stewardship and dominion over the world and other life forms, this does not mean that humans should dominate these forms of life.

Main facts

- The 1988 Papal Encyclical Sollicitudo Rei Socialis (On Social Concerns) stated that: 'The earth and all life on it is a gift from God given us to share and develop, not to dominate and exploit.' It continues 'The goods of the earth and the beauties of nature are to be enjoyed and celebrated as well as consumed ...We must consider the welfare of future generations in our planning for and utilisation of the earth's resources.' The Pope was making it clear that the earth and all life are gifts from God which should be treated with respect.

- One of the ways in which Christians show their care and thankfulness for the environment is in worship. Harvest Thanksgiving is a modern Church festival which began in 1843. It is a thanksgiving for the harvest which is held at the same time as traditional harvest home celebrations.

- A statement from the World Council of Churches said that: 'The dignity of nature as creation needs to be bound up with our responsibility for the preservation of life.' This shows that protecting nature is part of human responsibility for preserving all life.

- In 1998 the European Christian Environmental Network (ECEN) was established to help the Churches of Europe to engage in a broad range of environmental work.

- Although they are not Christian organisations, some Christians have chosen to join groups such as Greenpeace or the WWF to work towards the protection of the environment and demonstrate their Christian stewardship.

- CAFOD and Christian Aid are two Christian charities that undertake conservation work to enable people in the developing world to be self-sufficient.

Remember

Just because people are not religious believers it does not mean that they are not concerned about the world and the environment.

Key words

Encyclical: a formal statement from the Pope.
Stewardship: looking after something for someone else.
Thanksgiving: a prayer or act of worship offering thanks to God.
World Council of Churches: a fellowship of 349 churches, denominations and Church fellowships in more than 110 countries and territories throughout the world, bringing together over 560 million Christians.

Key text

Sollicitudo Rei Socialis
– Papal Encyclical which considers the environment

1.1 Roles of men and women in the Christian and Church family

There are still Christians, and Christian denominations, who believe that a woman should stay at home and care for the children and her husband. However, most people would probably take the view in Paul's epistle (letter) to the Galatians that all Christians are equal whether male or female.

Main facts

- In the first creation story in Genesis it says '… God created man in his own image, in the image of God he created him; male and female he created them' (Genesis 1:26–27).
- In the second creation story in Genesis, man was created first and then woman was created as a companion and helpmate to man. Some Christians might use this story to argue that women have a lesser, or at least different, role to men.
- In the Old Testament many women are seen as strong and important people and rulers.
- Jesus' attitude towards women in the gospel accounts shows him treating women as equals.
- In the New Testament there are examples of women such as Priscilla and Lydia who appear to be in positions of authority within the early Church.
- Some of the Free Churches have had women ministers since the nineteenth century: the first female Methodist minister was ordained in 1880. The Anglican Church ordained its first women priests in 1974 in the USA and 1994 in Britain.
- The first woman bishop was the Reverend Barbara C. Harris who was consecrated as a bishop in the Episcopal Church in Boston, USA in 1989. However, the Anglican Church is still debating whether women can become bishops.
- Neither the Roman Catholic nor Orthodox Churches allow women to be ordained. The reasons given are that Jesus only chose men to be his disciples and at the Eucharist the priest represents Jesus.

Key words

Creation stories: the two accounts of creation in Genesis.
Free Churches: Churches which are separate from government and the 'established church' (Church of England).
New Testament: the second part of the Christian Bible.
Old Testament: the first part of the Christian Bible, originally the Tenakh – Jewish Scriptures.
Ordained: an officially appointed priest or minister.
Orthodox Churches: the Eastern Christian Churches that are in full communion with the Ecumenical Patriarchate of Constantinople and with each other.
Roman Catholic Church: the world's largest Christian Church which is governed by the Pope.

Key people

Adam – the first human being
Deborah – an Old Testament prophetess
Delilah – the wife of Samson in the Old Testament who brought about his capture through cutting his hair
Eve – the first female
Jael – a heroine from the Old Testament who kills an enemy of Israel
Lydia – a convert of St Paul in the New Testament
Priscilla – one of the important women in the early Church
Queen of Sheba – an important ruler who travelled to see King Solomon

Remember

Even in the twenty-first century there are still many arguments and discussions about the roles of men and women. This can be over particular religious issues, such as whether women can be ordained in the Church, or other non-religious issues such as whether women should stay at home and care for their family.

Key texts

Genesis 1–3 – the two creation stories and the Fall
Luke 8:43–48 – Jesus heals the woman who has been bleeding for 12 years. She is healed through faith
Galatians 3:28–29 – Paul taught that everyone was equal in Christ

1.2 Marriage and marriage ceremonies

Marriage provides a relationship through which husband and wife support each other; this relationship is built on love and faithfulness. It also provides a secure environment for the bringing up of children.

Main facts

- Marriage is seen as a gift from God and part of God's plan for creation.
- The importance of marriage is stressed by Jesus: 'Therefore what God has joined together, let man not separate' and these words are stated in the marriage ceremony.
- The words of the marriage ceremony stress that the promises of the bride and groom are made before God.
- At the beginning of the service the priest or minister reminds the couple of the seriousness of marriage. They are told that it symbolises the relationship between Christ and the Church and that a marriage was the occasion of Jesus' first miracle.
- The couple answers these vows: Will you love her/him, comfort her/him, honour and protect her/him, and, forsaking all others, be faithful to her/him as long as you both shall live?
- They promise that they will stay together: for better, for worse, for richer, for poorer, in sickness and in health, to love and to cherish, till death us do part; according to God's holy law.
- The couple may exchange rings. The circle represents eternity and their unending love for each other.
- One of the most important aspects of a Christian marriage is that, for Roman Catholics and the Orthodox Church, it is regarded as a sacrament: an outward visible sign of an inward spiritual grace.
- In a Roman Catholic marriage the service is followed by a special Eucharist called a nuptial mass.

Remember

The Christian Church believes that it is a sin for people to have sexual relations with each other unless they are married because of the vow to be faithful taken before God. Some Christians believe sexual relations before marriage also break the seventh commandment 'do not commit adultery'.

Key words

Eucharist: a Christian sacrament that commemorates the Last Supper, with the priest or minister consecrating bread and wine that is consumed by the congregation.

Nuptial mass: a special Eucharist celebrated at a wedding.

Sacrament: an outward, physical sign of an inward, invisible grace. The Roman Catholic and Orthodox Churches recognise seven sacraments.

Vows: promises made between the couple getting married with God as a witness.

Key texts

Mark 10:6–9 – Jesus states that divorce is wrong

John 2:1–11 – the first miracle: Jesus changes water into wine at the wedding in Cana

1.3 Christian responses to civil partnerships

The reaction of the Churches to civil partnerships is based on biblical teaching where it appears that homosexual activity is condemned in both the Old and New Testaments. Examples are the destruction of Sodom and Gomorrah and Paul's teachings in 1 Corinthians.

Main facts

- On 5 December 2005 civil partnerships became legal in the UK.
- Civil partnership services are formal ceremonies for same-sex couples in which they make promises to each other and which gives them the same legal status as married heterosexual couples.
- Civil partnership ceremonies, by law, do not have any religious content to them.
- The Roman Catholic Church and Church of England are opposed to civil partnerships because they teach that marriage is the proper place for sexual activity to occur and that one of the main purposes of sex should be to create a new life which homosexual sex cannot do.
- The Roman Catholic Church sees homosexual activity as essentially being masturbation, which it believes is always wrong because it is misuse of the sexual genitalia and is seen as the sin of Onan.
- The Methodist Church has always been open to discussion of homosexuality but states that it: 'does not consider that homosexual genital practice [homosexual sex] … is acceptable'. So although they accept a person as being homosexual they would condemn the person acting on homosexual instincts. The Church will not bless civil partnerships.
- Only the Religious Society of Friends (Quakers) fully accepts homosexual couples in their meetings. Quakers would support a couple who had entered into a civil partnership.
- Individual Christians may have quite different opinions to the Churches. They may feel that everyone is created in God's image and that therefore they are equal and should be treated equally.

Key words

Civil partnership: the legal ceremony in which two people of the same sex become married.

Heterosexual: someone who has a sexual attraction to people of the opposite sex.

Homosexual: someone who has a sexual attraction to a member of the same sex.

Key people

Onan – Old Testament figure whose sin of 'spilling his seed on the ground' is condemned by God

Paul – one of the first Christians, converted to following Christ by a spiritual encounter on the road to Damascus

Remember

Over the years the attitude of the Christian Church has changed. However, the majority of the Christian Churches would say that while homosexual feelings are acceptable because the person can do nothing about them, nevertheless they must live celibate lives because homosexual activity is always a sin.

Key texts

Genesis 19:4–5 – the story of the destruction of Sodom and Gomorrah
Genesis 38:6–10 – the sin of Onan
Leviticus 18:22 – homosexuality is condemned
1 Corinthians 6:9–10 – Paul condemns homosexuality

1.4 Christian beliefs about divorce and remarriage

Christians see marriage as being for life and consider that the promises the couple made were to God as well as to each other. Because of this divorce is always viewed very seriously. However, Christians have different attitudes on the subject of divorce.

Main facts

- Divorce is not welcomed in the teachings of the Old Testament:
  - Moses taught that divorce was permitted if a man found out something indecent about his wife.
  - In Malachi, God says 'I hate divorce'.
- In the Sermon on the Mount, Jesus said that divorce was wrong and that the Old Testament rules about divorce were not strict enough.
- However, Jesus said that adultery was grounds for divorce.
- In 1981 the Church of England decided that although a person had been divorced this should not prevent them from marrying someone else in a church ceremony.
- The Orthodox Church does allow divorced people to marry a second or third time. These marriages are performed by 'economy' – out of concern for the spiritual well-being of the people involved.
- The Roman Catholic Church accepts that people may get a divorce, which is a civil matter, but they are still seen as married because a sacrament cannot be undone. If they have a sexual relationship with another person or get married again in a civil ceremony they are not allowed to receive communion as what they are doing is seen as a sin.
- In certain circumstances, the Pope may grant an annulment to a couple who wish to divorce. An annulment says that the original marriage was flawed and therefore did not actually take place. This only happens in certain circumstances: for example, if the couple were not mentally fit to understand the seriousness of marriage. Once an annulment has been granted the couple are free to marry again in church.

Key words

Adultery: when someone who is married has a sexual relationship with someone to whom they are not married.
Annulment: a declaration that a marriage was never a proper marriage in the eyes of the Church, e.g. because one of the parties was not completely committed to it.
Economy: an act which is done out of concern for others.

Key person

Pope – the spiritual head of the Roman Catholic Church and, as such, God's representative on earth. He can proclaim whether or not a marriage took place

Remember

In most Christian Churches divorce is permitted, although Christians believe that they should do everything they can to try to help the couple stay together, such as going to marriage counselling (Relate), praying, or speaking to the priest or minister.

Key text

Matthew 5:31–32 – Jesus' teaching on divorce in the Sermon on the Mount

1.5 Christian beliefs about sexual relationships

Even though many people now choose to live together in relationships without being married, this is not welcomed by the Christian Church.

- Christianity teaches that the sexual act must take place exclusively within marriage. In Genesis 2:24 men and women are told to 'become one flesh'. Outside of marriage sexual activity always constitutes a grave sin.
- St Paul remained unmarried and appears to have thought that the ideal was for everyone to be celibate. This might have been because he believed people should not be diverted away from following Jesus.
- Some scholars have suggested that Paul thought that Jesus' return – the second coming or Parousia – would happen very soon and that people should stay celibate and wait for this.
- In the Roman Catholic Church, priests are required to take a vow of celibacy as the Church believes that if a priest was married he would be distracted from loving and serving God.
- Agape – a non-sexual love which is completely selfless and spiritual is shown in the teachings of the New Testament. Agape, as distinct from physical love, is the unconditional love exemplified by Jesus' sacrifice on the cross. It is given to everyone no matter who they are, what they have done or whether they return that love.
- The Christian Churches are all opposed to adultery, fornication and, with few exceptions, homosexuality. They view all of these as going against the unitive and creative purpose of sex within marriage. Some Churches are prepared to allow cohabiting couples into their congregations but the majority will not.

Remember

The seventh commandment, 'You shall not commit adultery' is often interpreted as it being wrong to have a sexual relationship with anyone to whom you are not married, even if you are not married.

Key texts

Matthew 5:27–28 – Jesus says that adultery is wrong but thinking lustfully about someone is just as bad
1 Corinthians 6:19–20 – Paul says that casual sex is wrong because the body is a temple for the Holy Spirit
1 Corinthians 7:1–9 – Paul says that it is better to get married than indulge in casual sex
1 John 4:7–12 – this letter outlines Christian love

Key words

Agape: selfless love, taught by Jesus of Nazareth and felt by Christians for their fellow human beings.
Celibate: someone who abstains from sexual activity.
Chastity: abstaining from sexual activity because of religious vows, e.g. a nun or monk.
Cohabitation: to live together without being formally married.
Fornication: sexual activity between two adults who are not married to each other.
Parousia (second coming): the anticipated and prophesied return of Jesus Christ to judge humanity at the end of the world.

1.6 Christian beliefs about contraception

Christians believe that life is a gift from God and sacred, and that the purpose of sexual activity is to create new life. Because of this the Roman Catholic Church does not approve of artificial contraception. Some other Churches accept the use of artificial contraception in order to ensure children are planned and wanted.

Main facts

- Although there are no specific teachings within the Bible about contraception, Christians believe that life is a gift from God and sacred and therefore many of them feel that contraception (or birth control) is preventing a new life which God wishes to be born and is therefore a sin.
- Many others believe that the Bible should be interpreted for the age in which Christians live. Although they think that the teachings on life being sacred within the Bible should be considered carefully, because the world is becoming overpopulated and there is a great deal of poverty, they believe contraception should be allowed.
- The Roman Catholic Church considers that conception is a natural outcome of sexual intercourse and that anything which prevents this is wrong. It teaches that married couples have an obligation to obey God's command to Adam and Eve to 'Be fruitful and increase in number'.
- The only form of contraception which is permitted by the Roman Catholic Church is the 'rhythm method' sometimes called 'natural family planning', or fertility awareness. This involves planning sex around the most infertile times in a woman's monthly cycle.
- The Anglican Church teaches that decisions about the number of children in a family and when to have them is a matter for the parents' conscience which is influenced by God.
- The Orthodox Churches do not have a single view about contraception except that abortifacients such as the morning-after pill are not permitted.

Key words

Abortifacient: a drug or device that causes an abortion.
Artificial contraception: medicine or devices which prevent conception.
Contraception: also known as birth control and fertility control, uses methods or devices to prevent pregnancy. These may include artificial methods such as condoms or natural controls such as the rhythm method.
Natural contraception: techniques such as 'natural family planning'.
Rhythm method: now often referred to as 'natural family planning' – planning sex around the most infertile times in a woman's monthly cycle.

Remember

There are different types of contraception. Natural contraception uses techniques such as natural family planning or the rhythm method to avoid a woman becoming pregnant. Artificial contraception uses medicines or devices to present conception occurring.

Key text

Genesis 1:26–27 – God made humans in his own image

2.1 Core Christian beliefs about the nature of human life

To understand Christian views on the issues of abortion, euthanasia and suicide you need to first understand some important Christian beliefs.

Main facts

Key Christian beliefs:

- **That human life is sacred and holy.** This is summed up in the phrase 'the sanctity of life'.
- **That humans have a soul.** The soul is a spiritual part of our being that lives on after death. It is the soul that makes humans different from animals.
- **That God has a plan for each person.** They should trust God's plan.
- **That Jesus shows people how we should behave.** Christians believe that Jesus was God in human form. So by his life and his actions (as described in the New Testament) they can see what God wants them to do.

Christians who believe this should:

- **Look after others** – if all are made in God's image then all should be valued and cared for.
- **Look after themselves** – living healthy and pure lives – if you are made in God's image, or like a temple for God's presence you want to keep yourself fit for God.
- **Resist those that are damaging what God has created** – if Christians see others damaging human life in any way they will speak up and try to challenge this behaviour.

Key words

Sanctity of life: the belief that there is something special or holy about life.
Soul: the non-physical part of a person which may go to heaven when the person dies.

Key texts

Genesis 1:26–27 – God made humans in his own image
Genesis 2:7 – God gives Adam the 'breath of life'
Exodus 20:13 – 'Do not murder'
1 Corinthians 3:16–17 – 'the body is a temple of the Holy Spirit'
Matthew 25:35 and 25:40 – 'When I was thirsty you gave me something to drink …'
Psalm 139:13–16 – humans are wonderfully made

2.2 Attitudes to abortion

Abortion is the induced termination of a pregnancy to destroy the foetus. Key questions for Christians when it comes to thinking about abortion are: 'when does life begin?' and 'who should make the decision?'

Main facts

- Roman Catholics believe that the killing of an unborn baby is morally wrong in all circumstances. They believe that life begins at conception and that the unborn baby has the same right to life as its mother. Some Christians believe that an embryo or foetus is only a 'potential person'. Others believe that it becomes a person when it is capable of surviving on its own.
- Though Roman Catholics believe that the killing of an unborn baby is morally wrong, if abortion is needed to save the mother's life, such as in the case of an ectopic pregnancy, they would accept the doctrine of double effect. This says that if doing something morally good has a morally bad side-effect, it is right to do it providing the bad side-effect was not intended even though it was known.
- The Church of England also opposes abortion but recognises that there can be certain conditions when abortion would be morally acceptable such as the child would experience a low quality of life due to severe medical disabilities, or in the case of rape.
- The Methodist Church says that abortion is always an evil but recognises that there are cases where abortion may be the lesser of two evils: if the child would be born with an incurable disease for example.
- Some Christians are more willing to accept early abortions than those which take place later in a pregnancy.

Key words

Abortion: the induced termination of a pregnancy. Sometimes called a 'procured' or 'direct' abortion.
Doctrine of double effect: if doing something morally good has a morally bad side-effect, it is right to do it providing the bad side-effect was not intended.
Ectopic pregnancy: when a foetus starts to grow in a Fallopian tube rather than the womb.
Miscarriage: when a baby is aborted through natural causes. Sometimes called a spontaneous abortion.

Remember

Many of the Christian Churches have a relative morality in their approach to abortion – they adapt the rules to different situations but would still see abortion as a last resort. The most common secular (non-religious) view is that the woman should have the right to choose an abortion herself if she wishes it after counselling, as she has the right over her own body. A secular approach would usually consider that the foetus is not a person until some time into its development (usually 22 weeks). However, some people hold different views as to when a foetus becomes a person, such as conception, when brain activity starts, when the foetus becomes recognisable in the womb, when it moves, when it is viable, at birth.

Key texts

Exodus 20:13 – 'Do not murder'
Psalm 139:13–16 – God creates people in the womb

2.3 Christian attitudes to fertility treatment

There are many couples who, through no fault of their own, cannot conceive and have children. Two religious and ethical issues that arise from fertility treatment are whether humans have the right to create life and what happens to the embryos created during the process.

Main facts

There are different forms of fertility treatment:
- Use of drugs to make the woman more fertile.
- AIH: artificial insemination by the husband, where the husband's sperm is injected into the wife's reproductive tract.
- Donor insemination: where donor sperm is used instead because the husband is not fertile.
- IVF: *in vitro* fertilisation done outside the human body using the sperm of a husband or donor, and the egg of the wife or a donor egg.

The law now states that anyone donating sperm or eggs has to provide their details, so that at the age of eighteen a person conceived in this way can seek out their biological parents.

- The Human Fertilisation and Embryology Act 1990:
  - Frozen embryos may be stored for a maximum of ten years. However, these can only be implanted and used if both partners agree.
  - Scientific experiments may only be carried out on embryos up until fourteen days after conception; after this time they may not be kept alive.
- There are many Christians who, for different reasons, don't agree with fertility treatment. They might believe that only God should create life. This is part of the teaching about sanctity of life.
- Roman Catholics believe life begins at conception. This causes a major problem with fertility treatment (such as IVF) which can produce spare embryos which they believe goes against the sixth commandment.
- The Roman Catholic Church does not believe that having a baby is a God-given right but rather a divine gift.
- Also the Roman Catholic Church is opposed to donor insemination because they think that the introduction of a third party is a form of adultery.

Remember

Some people object to fertility treatment as it may be used by people who are in a homosexual relationship, or are not in a relationship at all but still want to have children, or have passed the natural age for child-bearing but still want to have a baby.

Key words

AIH: artificial insemination by husband.
Donor insemination: artificial insemination by donor.
IVF (*in vitro* fertilisation): when sperm and an egg are put together in a tube until an embryo is formed which is then transferred into a woman's womb.

Key texts

Genesis 1:28a – 'Be fruitful and increase in number'
Genesis 21:1–7 – God allows Sarah to have a baby

2.4 Christian attitudes to cloning

Cloning creates a genetically identical animal or plant from another. The most famous example of a cloned animal was Dolly the sheep (1997–2003). Plants are often cloned; when someone takes a cutting and grows another plant from it, they are producing a clone. Human identical twins are also clones of each other.

Main facts

- Most of the concerns about cloning relate to the possibility that it might be used to clone humans. Most Christians feel that the cloning of a human, were it to be possible, is unacceptable.
- Most countries have banned the use of cloning to produce human babies (human reproductive cloning).
- In therapeutic cloning (or cell nucleus replacement), tissues are created. Single cells are taken from a person and 'reprogrammed' to create stem cells, which have the potential to develop into any type of cell in the body in order to provide replacement organs or limbs. In 2001 the Human Fertilisation and Embryo Act allowed the use of human embryos in stem cell research, using leftover embryos from IVF treatment.
- Many Christians feel that research into therapeutic cloning is against the will of God as it is unnatural. They argue that each person has individuality given by God and that human life should not be tampered with – we should not 'play God'.
- Others would say that people have a God-given responsibility to care for creation and if therapeutic cloning would benefit humans it is a good thing as long as it is strictly controlled.
- The Roman Catholic Church teaches that cloning separates the procreation of children from the sexual act and often involves the creation and subsequent destruction of a large number of fertilised eggs. This is against Roman Catholic teaching on the sanctity of life.

Key words

Cloning: the making of a replica.
Reproductive cloning: cloning which creates offspring.
Stem cells: single cells which have the potential to be 'reprogrammed' to develop into any type of cell in the body.
Therapeutic cloning: a medical procedure where single cells are taken from a person or embryo and 'reprogrammed' to create stem cells which can be used in medical treatment.

Remember

Christian teaching about the sanctity of life says that humans are not tools for science, nor a means to an end, no matter how well intentioned the action.

2.5 Christian attitudes to suicide

Most Christians believe that it is wrong for a person to commit suicide, although they recognise that these people may have gone beyond the stage where they are able to think clearly.

Main facts

- Suicide: 'the ... act of taking one's own life, self-murder'. Although there has been a general drop in suicide rates, there has been a very significant increase in young people taking their own lives.
- By the nineteenth century, suicide was seen as the result of insanity rather than being simply a sin.
- Christians might argue against suicide by saying:
  - It is murdering yourself: the sixth commandment is 'You shall not murder' (Exodus 20:13).
  - It is deciding what only God can decide.
  - It is destroying God's temple.
  - It is ducking life's challenges.
  - It is selfish and devastating to others.
  - It is ignoring God's plan.
- In 1953 Chad Varah, an Anglican vicar in London, founded the organisation now known as the Samaritans. Anyone who is in emotional distress or contemplating suicide can call and speak to someone in complete confidence. The listeners are not counsellors and they do not offer advice.

Key words

Sin: an act which goes against God's wishes.
Suffering: physical, mental or spiritual pain.

Key person

Chad Varah (1911–2007) – a vicar who began the first telephone help-line which later grew into the Samaritans

Remember

Most Christians recognise that people who kill themselves are often suffering from depression and are not really in a fit state to think clearly. People who attempt suicide should be helped to overcome the reasons which made them want to kill themselves.

Key texts

Exodus 20:13 – 'Do not murder'
Ecclesiastes 3:1–3a – 'There is a time to live and a time to die'
1 Corinthians 6:19–20 – 'the body is a temple of the Holy Spirit'

2.6 Christian attitudes to euthanasia

Euthanasia means ending the life of someone who is suffering. There are different Christian attitudes and beliefs on whether or not the quality of life is more important than the sanctity of life.

Main facts

- There are three types of euthanasia:
  - Voluntary euthanasia (assisted suicide): the person concerned asks someone to help them die, perhaps by asking for assistance to take an overdose of painkillers.
  - Involuntary euthanasia: euthanasia carried out without the patient's consent, for example, if they are in a persistent vegetative state and no longer able to live without a life-support machine, which is then switched off.
- Euthanasia can be passive, involving the withholding of food or common treatments which are necessary for life to continue or active which usually involves the use of drugs to end life.
- The Roman Catholic Church is totally opposed to euthanasia. It believes that any act to deliberately end a life in this way constitutes murder and so breaks the sixth commandment. However, the Church accepts that there is a difference between deliberate killing and the shortening of life by pain-killing drugs.
- The Anglican Church has a similar view to the Roman Catholic Church. It teaches that although the deliberate taking of human life is forbidden, there are strong arguments that people should not be kept alive at all costs when they are suffering intolerable pain. To allow someone to die may be the most loving thing to do.
- The Religious Society of Friends (Quakers) does not have a united view on euthanasia. For Quakers what is important is that they do the most loving thing.
- Quality of life versus sanctity of life? Many Christians and non-believers would wish to consider the quality of life of the patient. Christians in particular would want to compare this with teachings about the sanctity of life: should a patient be forced to live even though they are in desperate pain which cannot be relieved?

Key words

Euthanasia: a gentle or easy death; helping someone to die.
Hospice: a place where terminally-ill patients are cared for.
Palliative care: care given to a terminally ill patient to help them die in as much comfort as possible.

Key person

Cicely Saunders (1918–2005) – founded the first modern hospice, St Christopher's in London, in 1967

2.7 Christian beliefs about the use of animals in medical research

Many Christians would follow their individual consciences as to whether or not animals should be used in medical research. However, most Christians recognise that animals are part of God's creation and should be treated with care and not be hurt unnecessarily.

Main facts

- The Bible teaches that humans have a role of stewardship over the earth and should care for it.
- In the past, animals were not considered as important as humans and many Christians do not believe animals have souls or can have a relationship with God.
- The Roman Catholic Church and the Anglican Church both consider animal experimentation as an important method of testing for life-saving drugs but the animals must not be hurt unnecessarily.
- In the past, medical experiments on animals have produced a vaccine for polio, assisted in the development of anaesthetics and helped to produce drugs for the treatment of asthma.
- The Religious Society of Friends (Quakers) are opposed to research on animals for trivial matters, such as cosmetics, but are divided on whether experiments should be done in order to save lives. They believe that to say you love God but then impose cruelty on his creations is a contradiction.
- However, many Christians do not approve of using animals in medical research. They believe God made his covenant with animals as well as humans and that both humans and animals have the same origin in God.
- So while many Christians would be happy to eat animals, as they are told to do in Peter's vision, they still believe that animals are God's creation and should not be allowed to suffer.
- St Francis of Assisi said that animals 'had the same source as [himself]'. Therefore inflicting pain on any living creature is incompatible with living in a Christ-like way.

Key people

Adam – the first human being who was given the task of stewardship of the earth and dominion over it

St Peter – had a vision of a sheet of food full of animals descending from heaven

St Francis of Assisi (1181–1226) – believed that animals had souls

Remember

There are no specific passages in the Bible about animal testing but many Christians will refer to passages from Genesis about stewardship and dominion to support their opinions.

Key words

Dominion: authority or rule.
Medical research: scientific experiments carried out to help cure disease.
Stewardship: looking after something for someone else.

Key texts

Genesis 1:28 – Adam is told to rule over the earth
Genesis 2:15 – Adam is told to 'take care of' the earth
Acts 10:10–15 – Peter's vision which told Peter to kill and eat animals

3.1 Christian views about wealth

The Christian Churches have spoken out about the way in which followers should use their money. Vatican II (the Second Vatican Council of the Roman Catholic Church) (1962–5) declared that the religious and the secular worlds all belonged to God without separation and that faith and justice were linked together. Therefore the right use of wealth is important to God in ensuring justice for everyone.

Main facts

- As the world appears to become smaller, with business being conducted on a global basis, it seems that people become ever more concerned with having as much money as they possibly can. Christians believe people should be more concerned about gaining spiritual gifts in heaven.
- The Roman Catholic Church says: 'Rich nations have a grave moral responsibility towards those which are unable to ensure the means of their development by themselves.'
- The Church of England teaches 'that, as a matter of common humanity and of our mutual interest in survival, the world requires a new and more equitable system of economic relationships between nations'.

Key words

Faith: belief in something without having proof.
Justice: fairness in the way people are treated.
Poverty: not having enough money for basic needs.
Wealth: money or possessions.

Remember

Fairness and justice for everyone, especially the poor, is one of the main teachings of Jesus and of Christianity.

Key texts

Genesis 28:22 – Jacob states he will give the Lord one tenth of everything
Matthew 6:1–4 – Jesus taught you should give to charity in secret
Luke 21:1–4 – Jesus praising the poor widow who put in all she had in the charity box
1 John 3:17 – a person cannot love God if they do not show care and concern for others
1 Corinthians 16:2 – if someone does not love God then they are cursed

3.2 Christian views on the causes of hunger, poverty and disease

In the past many people believed that suffering was punishment from God. However, one of the central beliefs of Christianity is that God is all good. Today Christians have found different reasons for why people suffer.

Main facts

- There are many different reasons why some people are so poor and live such terrible lives. These include debt, corrupt governments, war, etc. At the time of Jesus many people believed that illness and suffering were punishments for sin or a lack of faith in God.
- In the Middle Ages the plague was considered to be a punishment for the sins of the world. Even recently, some religious leaders from across the world referred to HIV/AIDS as the 'gay plague' and said that it was God's righteous judgement on homosexuals. After the Asian Boxing Day tsunami of 2004, there was a Christian website in America which had a banner proclaiming: 'Thank God for the tsunami because it has killed so many homosexuals'.
- Many of the instances of the poverty in the developing world have been caused by the way in which these countries were exploited for their wealth and natural resources by the rich countries of the north in the north–south divide.
- It is not easy for Christians to explain or understand the natural disasters of famine, drought, floods and hurricanes which bring so much death and misery. In the past it was thought that natural disasters were the work of the Devil. Some people believed that the Devil brought disasters on to people to test their faith.
- Another view was that God allowed the Devil to tempt people in this way in order to show how strong their faith was. An example of this can be found in the Book of Job where the Devil is often referred to as the 'Adversary'.

Key word

Omnibenevolence: all-good.

Key person

Job – a character in the Old Testament who is tested by the Devil to see if he would lose his faith in God

Remember

In 1948, the General Assembly of the United Nations (UN) signed the Universal Declaration of Human Rights. This declaration clearly establishes the basic rights to which every human being is entitled and which the member countries of the UN would work to establish. The First Article of the Declaration is particularly important: 'All human beings are born free and equal in dignity and rights. They are endowed with reason and conscience and should act towards one another in a spirit of brotherhood.' This is found in the Christian message 'As I have loved you, so you must love one another' (John 13:34b).

Key texts

Genesis 1:26–27 – God made humans in his own image
Job 1:12 – when God tells the Adversary (Devil) he may test Job
Mark 12:31a – love your neighbour as yourself
Luke 5:18–25 – Jesus heals the paralysed man who is sick because of his sins

3.3 Biblical teaching about caring for others

Teachings about caring for the poor, the starving and the sick, the outcasts of society, are found in throughout the Bible and are central to Christian belief. Luke's gospel is particularly concerned with the outcasts of society and how Jesus lived and taught among them.

Main facts

Christian responses to the needs of the starving, poor and sick are based on the teachings in the Bible about care for others:

- The Book of Leviticus teaches people to help the poor and support them. It also says that money should be lent to the poor without interest.
- When Jesus was asked what was the most important commandment he said: 'The most important one … is this: "Hear, O Israel, the Lord our God, the Lord is one. Love the Lord your God with all your heart and with all your soul and with all your mind and with all your strength." The second is this: "Love your neighbour as yourself." There is no commandment greater than these' (Mark 12:28–31). For Christians this teaching means they should always care for others.
- In the Sermon on the Plain Jesus taught: 'Blessed are you who are poor, for yours is the kingdom of God. Blessed are you who hunger now, for you will be satisfied' (Luke 6:20b–21). Some people have said that in the sermon Jesus appears to be talking to people about future happiness and not an improvement in their present lives. The important point is that Jesus was promising that the situation of people who were suffering would improve. Christians believe that they have a duty to help bring in the Kingdom of God, and caring for others is one way to do this.
- Christian charities work to help those who are poor and suffering so that their lives on earth are improved.
- Many Christians try to follow the example set by Jesus when he healed the sick.
- Many Christians believe that prayer is an important aspect of caring for the poor.

Remember

In Luke's gospel, Jesus explained his mission to help the poor: 'The Spirit of the Lord is on me, because he has anointed me to preach good news to the poor' (Luke 4:18). Therefore, Christians believe they should follow the example of Jesus and help the poor through living and teaching the word of the Gospel.

Key texts

Leviticus 25:35–37 – interest should not be charged
Mark 12:28–31 – the two Great Commandments
Luke 4:18–19 – Jesus came to preach good news to the poor
Luke 6:20b–21 – Jesus taught that the poor are blessed because they will enter the kingdom of heaven

Key words

Interest: payment for borrowing money.
Kingdom of God: Jesus preached about the Kingdom of God, a time when everyone would live in harmony according to God's teachings.
Outcasts: people rejected by society.

3.4 Christian teachings on the use of money

Christians' concern for the poor also influences how they should spend their money. They do not believe that money is evil in itself but if someone puts their desires to be rich before carrying out the wishes of God to look after the poor then this becomes evil. Jesus explained this in the Parable of the Rich Man and Lazarus.

Main facts

- In the first century CE many people believed that wealth was a gift from God and Jesus warned them against keeping the money to themselves. This teaching can be found in the Parable of the Rich Fool.
- This message is repeated in Matthew's gospel when Jesus says: 'You cannot serve both God and Money.'
- Jesus was clear that people who wished to follow God should give away their riches: 'It is easier for a camel to go through the eye of a needle than for a rich man to enter the kingdom of God' (Luke 18:25). Some have interpreted this teaching as meaning that people should give away everything in order to follow Jesus' teachings. Examples of this are found in monks and nuns who live in communities without possessions of their own and take a vow of poverty. This vow of poverty can be seen as a way of working towards perfection as a Christian. Some people have interpreted this teaching as meaning that a person can be rich as long as they do not allow material wealth to come between them and their love of God and his teachings to help the poor.
- In Christianity there is also a principle called affective poverty which is when someone can separate themselves from any money or possessions which they have. The Church values relative property but not poverty where people do not have enough money to live.
- Paul taught that the 'love of money is the root of all evil' and Jesus said that people cannot serve two masters, God and money.
- Some Christians believe it is wrong for someone who is a Christian to be rich when there are people who are starving because of lack of money.
- Exodus (22:25) teaches that money should not be lent at interest.
- Many Christians do not approve of gambling, for example they may not agree to raffles to raise money. Reference to this can be found in Luke 19:45–46 where Jesus throws the money lenders out of the temple.

Key words

Absolute poverty: when someone does not have enough to buy even the essentials to live such as food and shelter.

Relative poverty: when someone does not have enough money to buy luxury items and is considered to be poor compared with other people in that society.

Remember

There is no Christian teaching against people having wealth provided they also help the poor and do not allow money to come between them and God.

Key texts

Proverbs 30:8–9 – teaching on riches and poverty
Matthew 6:24–31 – you cannot serve two masters – God and money
Luke 16:19–31 – the Parable of the Rich Man and Lazarus
Luke 18:25 – money should not be the main focus in life
1 Timothy 6:10 – the love of money is the root of all evil

3.5 How Christians should care for the poor

Jesus was concerned that people should always think of the well-being of others: 'Love your neighbour as yourself.' Christians see this as meaning that they should be charitable in their approach to other people.

Main facts

- Jesus' most famous teaching about caring for others is found in the Parable of the Sheep and the Goats in Matthew 25: 'For I was hungry and you gave me something to eat, I was thirsty and you gave me something to drink, I was a stranger and you invited me in, I needed clothes and you clothed me, I was sick and you looked after me, I was in prison and you came to visit me.' So Christians would help others because, as Blessed Mother Teresa said, 'within everyone is Christ', and therefore they would be helping Christ.
- When the Christian Church formed in Jerusalem it adopted Jesus' teachings:
  - 'All the believers were together and had everything in common. Selling their possessions and goods, they gave to anyone as he had need.'
  - 'All the believers were one in heart and mind. ... they shared everything they had. ... There were no needy persons among them.'
  The actions of the early Church should encourage Christians today to share with one another.
- Until 1936, many people in England paid tithes (a tenth of their income) to their parish church. Nowadays most church services have collections for charity work and for the church itself.
- There are many Christian charities who try to help those who are starving and suffering from hardship and diseases and also try to create a fairer distribution of wealth. Christian Aid, CAFOD and Tearfund are just three of the charities which aim to co-ordinate the work of the Churches and help the poor in accordance with Christian teachings. The work of these charities can be either short-term aid in the event of disasters or long-term aid which helps the people to achieve self-sufficiency.
- Christians believe that there are many ways in which they can help the poor either through the giving of money to charity or the giving of their talents, such as expertise or time.

> **Remember**
>
> Many Christians believe they should follow the example of Jesus and the early Church in helping the poor.

> **Key texts**
>
> **Matthew 25:31–46** – the Parable of the Sheep and the Goats teaches how people should treat others
> **Luke 12:15–17** – Jesus taught that earthly money was for earthly things but that God was more important
> **Acts 2:44–45; 4:32, 34–35** – the early Church sharing their possessions

Key words

Charity: money or help which is given voluntarily.
Parables: stories told by Jesus which have a moral message.

3.6 Christian teaching about moral and immoral occupations

There is very little specific teaching within Christianity about what is a moral or an immoral occupation. However, all Christians have a duty not to harm others and therefore they should not earn money in a way which has a bad or negative effect on other people. A Christian should look to their conscience and the teachings in the Bible before deciding what job to do.

Main facts

- Christians should do nothing to harm others, therefore some would not want to work in occupations such as the armed forces or be involved in the buying or selling of weapons.
- Christians should not be involved in illegal occupations such as prostitution, pornography or illegal drugs.
- Some Christian doctors and nurses may not want to take part in an abortion.
- The Methodist Church and the Salvation Army are opposed to the use of alcohol and would not want to be involved in its production or distribution, but neither of them try to force this view on other people.
- Some Christians would find working on Sunday difficult because of their beliefs about Sunday being a day of rest and of worship.
- The lending of money at interest produces different responses from Christian groups. This may be due, in part, to different teachings found in the Bible. Comparing teachings from different parts of the Bible might suggest that, whereas the Old Testament does not approve of lending money at interest, Jesus thought that it was acceptable. This can be seen by comparing the teaching in Exodus 22 with the Parable of the Talents.
- Christians might believe that helping others in such occupations as being a nurse, policeman, civil rights activist, etc. would be a good occupation because of Jesus' commandment to love one another.
- Christians might become involved in helping to care for the environment (stewardship) because of the teaching in Genesis 2.

Remember

Moral occupations are easier to explain than immoral ones. Most Christians would believe that any job which helped others, such as working in medicine or caring for the less fortunate, was moral. In other cases however, such as being a member of the armed forces, Christians may need to consider their conscience and the teachings of the Bible and the Church as to whether an occupation is immoral.

Key texts

Exodus 20:8 – 'keep the Sabbath holy' so Christians would not work on Sundays
Exodus 22:25 – 'charge no interest' – help others without causing them any further hardship
Matthew 25:14–30 – Parable of the Talents: God does not want people to waste their talents
1 Corinthians 3:16 – 'the body is a temple of the Holy Spirit'

Key words

Immoral: an action which is considered to be sinful.
Moral: an action which is considered to be good and following the way of Christ.
Vocation: a calling from God.

4.1 Christian attitudes to war: Holy war

Many Christians are pacifists but many wars have been fought in the name of Christianity.

Main facts

- In the past 100 years there have been very few days when war was not being fought somewhere in the world. All wars are the attempt of one power to defend itself against another or to take something from another group – this may be as fundamental as people's freedom.
- Christian teachings have been used to support both Holy war and the 'just war' theory (see page 61).
- Holy war is an argument that it can sometimes be necessary and right to use physical violence in order to defend a religion. Not all denominations agree with the idea of Holy war although there are examples in the Bible such as Joshua and the Battle of Jericho. The most significant Holy wars which involved Christianity were the Crusades.
- From 1101 to 1271 there were nine crusades. These were largely based on the belief of Christian Europe that it should take back the Holy Land and in particular Jerusalem from the Muslims who ruled it. These battles were often unsuccessful and frequently the crusaders did not even reach the Holy Land.
- The Albigensian or Cathar Crusade (1209–29) was fought by the Roman Catholic Church against a Christian group it considered to be heretical (it did not hold traditional Christian beliefs). Many atrocities were carried out against the Cathars.
- Most of the Christian Churches would not now support a Holy war.

Key words

Crusades: military expeditions fought from the eleventh to thirteenth centuries when Christians gathered together under a Holy banner to fight to regain Jerusalem and the Holy Land.
Holy war: war which is fought over religious issues by people who believe that this is what God wants.

Remember

Christian attitudes towards warfare, and in particular the idea of Holy war, have changed over the centuries.

4.2 Christian attitudes to war: the 'just war' theory

The idea of a 'just war' which is fought according to particular conditions developed from the ideas of Cicero (106–43BCE), Thomas Aquinas (1224–74) and Hugo Grotius (1583–1645). There are three criteria: *Jus ad bellum, jus in bello, jus post bellum*.

Main facts

- *Jus ad bellum*: rules which state whether it is right to go to war.
  - There must be a just cause for going to war.
  - The injustices suffered by one group must clearly be greater than those of the other group.
  - Only a legitimate authority can start the war.
  - The war must be fought with the right intention – material gain is not a just purpose.
  - There must be a reasonable chance of success.
  - Force must be a last resort after all peaceful means and negotiations have failed.
  - The hoped for benefits of the war must be greater than the probable evil and harm it will cause.
- *Jus in bello*: rules which define the correct conduct in war.
  - War must only be fought against enemy soldiers, and civilians must be protected.
  - The force used should be proportional to the wrong that has been done and the possible good which may come from the war.
  - Minimum force should be used to limit unnecessary death and destruction.
- *Jus post bellum*: rules which state how peace must be established after a war.
  - There should be just cause to end the war: the wrong has been righted and the enemy is ready to negotiate surrender. Or a war may be ended if it is clear it cannot be won.
  - There must be no revenge taken.
  - Peace terms must be made and accepted by legitimate authorities.
  - The victor must ensure that any punishment is limited to the people who were directly responsible for the conflict.
  - Any terms of surrender must be proportional to the original reason for the war.

Key people

Cicero (106–43BCE) – a Roman philosopher who put forward rules on how and why to fight war

Thomas Aquinas (1225–74) – a Christian theologian who proposed a version of the 'just war' theory so that Christians could fight in wars

Hugo Grotius (1583–1645) – a Dutch philosopher who laid down conditions for war

Remember

For a conflict to be considered a 'just war' all the conditions must be met. Many people would argue that the Second World War was a 'just war' but others would state that the *Jus in bello* condition to use only minimum force was violated in the bombing of Dresden.

Key words

Jus ad bellum: rules which state whether it is right to go to war.
Jus in bello: rules which define the correct conduct in war.
Jus post bellum: rules which state how peace must be established after a war.

4.3 Christian attitudes towards violence and pacifism

Christianity teaches that people should work towards a peaceful world and that fighting is always essentially evil. While some may feel that there are occasions when a war is just, others, such as members of the Religious Society of Friends (Quakers), are pacifists and may become conscientious objectors.

Main facts

- Many people believe that all war and fighting are wrong regardless of the purpose or eventual outcome. These people would be considered pacifists.
- Christian pacifists argue that the Christian principle of agape – selfless love – means that violence is never acceptable.
- One of the best-known groups of pacifists is the Religious Society of Friends (Quakers) who believe that any type of violence is wrong because they see God within every living being and to harm anyone harms God.
- There are sometimes occasions when pacifists may feel that they have to use violence. An example of this was Dietrich Bonhoeffer's actions.
- There are many occasions in the New Testament when Jesus preaches about the need for peace, for example 'Blessed are the peacemakers, for they will be called children of God' (Matthew 5:9).
- Jesus was seen as a man of peace when he entered Jerusalem on a donkey. Also he will not allow violence to be used when he is arrested at Gethsemane – 'for all who draw the sword will die by the sword' (Matthew 26:52b).
- However, there are also occasions, such as when he throws the moneylenders out of the temple, when Jesus seems to be acting in a violent manner.
- The attitudes of the Christian Churches towards violence and pacifism are based on these biblical teachings.

Key words

Agape: selfless love, taught by Jesus and felt by Christians for their fellow human beings.

Conscientious objectors: people who refuse to join the armed forces because of their beliefs.

Pacifism: belief that all fighting is wrong.

Key people

Jesus – God, in his incarnation of Jesus, demonstrated through some of his actions how he came as a man of peace

Dietrich Bonhoeffer (1906–45) – a German theologian who was a pacifist yet became involved in the plot to kill Hitler because he knew the evil had to be stopped. He said God would judge him for his decision

Remember

Although many Christians will believe that Jesus was a pacifist because of his teachings and example, some might disagree because of the occasion in the temple when he drove out the moneylenders.

Key texts

Joel 3:9–11 – the prophet tells Israel to 'prepare for war'
Micah 4:2–5 – the prophet speaks of a time of peace
Matthew 5:43–45 – Jesus taught the Beatitudes in the Sermon on the Mount and said that people should not only love their neighbour but also their enemy
1 John 4:7 – this epistle teaches that people should love one another because love comes from God

4.4 Christian teachings on justice and the aims of punishment

The Christian concept of justice is based on teachings from both the Old and New Testaments and this concept affects their attitudes to punishment which they believe has four main aims.

Main facts

- Christianity teaches that justice is one of the Four Cardinal Virtues: prudence, temperance, fortitude and justice.
- The concept of God's justice is found in both Testaments of the Bible:
  - 'Your eyes are open to all the ways of men; you reward everyone according to his conduct and as his deeds deserve' (Jeremiah 32:19b). 'Anyone who does wrong will be repaid for his wrong, and there is no favouritism' (Colossians 3:25).
  - Both of these quotes show that God wants people to reward and punish justly as God would do.
- Many teachings on forgiveness are found in the New Testament. On the cross Jesus asked God to forgive the people who had crucified him. Jesus told Peter to forgive 'seventy times seven' and he also told the Parable of the Lost (Prodigal) Son who was forgiven by his father.
- Christians usually believe that the aims of punishment are:
  - Deterrence – this may be applied individually to deter the person from committing the same crime again, or generally to deter other people from doing the same thing again.
  - Protection – to protect society and innocent people from harm from others.
  - Retribution – so that society and the victims of crime can see that the person has been punished.
  - Reformation – to give the criminal the chance to reform and live a better life.
- In the Old Testament there are many examples of crimes for which the punishment is death and some Christians still believe that capital punishment is the only way to deal with the most serious of crimes.
- Many other Christians believe that Jesus' teachings of forgiveness and agape mean that all human life must be treated as sacred and that although criminals must be punished justly it can never be right to take a life as punishment.

Remember

Although Christianity teaches forgiveness, Christians also believe that people should be punished fairly for their crimes. Many Christians believe that Jesus' teachings of forgiveness and agape mean that all human life must be treated as sacred and that although criminals must be punished justly it can never be right to take a life as punishment.

Key texts

Jeremiah 32:19b – the prophet teaches that God rewards people for good deeds and punishes the ones who do bad deeds
Colossians 3:25 – no matter who it is, if someone does wrong they should be punished

Key words

Deterrence: when a punishment is designed to persuade other people not to do the same thing.
Four Cardinal Virtues: the four most important virtues or good actions which are prudence (carefulness); temperance (restraint or self-control); fortitude (courage or resilience) and justice (fair treatment).
Protection: when a criminal is put in jail so that the public are kept safe.
Reformation: punishment which will allow the criminal to become a better person.
Retribution: when the criminal is punished so as to bring a sense of justice to the injured party.

4.5 Christian responses to the treatment of criminals

Although Christians believe people should be punished appropriately for the crimes they have committed, they also think criminals should be forgiven for their wrongdoings and be restored to society after they have been punished. They think criminals should not be mistreated in prison as Jesus taught that everyone should be treated humanely.

Main facts

- Christianity teaches forgiveness for wrongdoings as this follows the example and teachings of Jesus. Jesus' teaching of forgiveness is found in many places, for example in the story of the woman caught in adultery (John 8:3–11).
- Forgiveness does not mean there should be no punishment. Christian teaching is that people should be punished fairly for their crimes. However, if they are truly repentant for what they have done and ask for forgiveness, then they should be forgiven after they have been punished.
- Many Christians are concerned over the way in which prisoners are treated, particularly in the severely overcrowded prisons of twenty-first century Britain. Christians are commanded by Jesus to care for the weak and prisoners.
- The Quaker, Elizabeth Fry (1780–1845) worked to improve prison conditions in the nineteenth century and this work is continued today by the Howard League for Penal Reform.
- Many Christians work with prisoners to help them lead better lives when they leave prison. They also visit them in prison in accordance with the teachings of the Parable of the Sheep and Goats (Matthew 25:31–46).

Key people

Jesus – taught that to sin is wrong but that God would forgive those who truly repent
John Howard (1726–90) – a man who helped to reform prisons
Elizabeth Fry (1780–1845) – a Quaker who devoted her life to making prisons a better place where people could have dignity and learn a trade

Remember

Although Jesus' message was one of love and forgiveness many Christians would say that Jesus was preaching a true justice so that people were not judged and punished by those who were themselves no better than the accused.

Key text

John 8:3–11 – Jesus protects the woman accused of adultery by reminding people that everyone sins and people should look to their own sins first before rushing to condemn others

4.6 Christian beliefs and responses to social injustice

The phrase 'social injustice' is often used when some people are seen to be discriminated against in a society and have fewer rights or benefits than others.

Main facts

- Social injustice covers areas such as poverty, racism, oppression by governments and unfair imprisonment.
- Christian teaching is that social injustice is wrong because all life was created by God and is therefore equally valuable to God and should be shown the same respect.
- Some Christians respond to social injustice by working with organisations such as the Salvation Army, Cancel the Debt campaign and campaigns against racism.
- Many Christians take positive action against social injustice by joining organisations designed to fight for social equality, such as Amnesty International.
- Liberation theology is a modern development in the Christian Church. It is particularly concerned with issues of equality for all, based on Jesus' teaching that he had come '... to release the oppressed' (Luke 4:18b).
- Liberation theology teaches that if the law of a country acts against the ordinary people in a way which can be seen as un-Christian, then it must be opposed and, if necessary, broken.
- The work of liberation theologians is seen most clearly in Latin America and in some parts of Asia and Africa.
- Two of the most famous priests of the liberation theology movement in the twentieth century were Father Camillo Torres who was shot dead in 1966 and Archbishop Óscar Romero who was killed in March 1980 while celebrating mass.

Key people

Óscar Romero (1917–80) – a Roman Catholic Archbishop of San Salvador who spoke out against how the government treated the poor, and organised Christians and the poor to speak out against the oppression in their country. He was shot in March 1980 while saying mass

Camillo Torres (1929–66) – a Roman Catholic priest in Colombia who took part in armed uprisings against the government to fight for justice for the poor. He left the Church because it did not support him. He was shot dead in 1966

Remember

Many Catholic leaders have criticised liberation theology for going too far and not upholding the laws of the land. They do not approve of the violence of some of the attacks and consider that there are other ways of working to help the poor which do not go against Christian teachings on peace.

Key words

Liberation theology: the movement, principally in South America, which tries to help the poor who are oppressed by social injustice.
Social injustice: unfair treatment of people in society. It can refer to issues such as racism, ageism, poverty, sexism, etc.

Key texts

Leviticus 19:33–34 – people should be kind to everyone, including foreigners, because the Israelites themselves had to go to Egypt in times of famine
Amos 2:6–7a – the prophet teaches that God will punish those who mistreat the poor
James 2:1–9 – God has no favourites and people should not treat a poor person any differently to a rich person

5.1 Principle of equality

The principle of equality is that everyone should be treated fairly without suffering prejudice or discrimination. The principle of equality for everyone is enshrined in the UN Universal Declaration of Human Rights.

Main facts

- The UN Universal Declaration of Human Rights states that everyone should have the same rights and freedoms whoever and wherever they are:
  - Article 1. All human beings are born free and equal in dignity and rights. They are endowed with reason and conscience and should act towards one another in a spirit of brotherhood.
  - Article 2. Everyone is entitled to all the rights and freedoms set forth in this Declaration, without distinction of any kind, such as race, colour, sex, language, religion, political or other opinion, national or social origin, property, birth or other status.
- However, people all over the world are not treated equally and fairly and suffer from prejudice and discrimination. This can be because of their race, sex, religion, colour, sexuality, age, disability, language, social class, or simply living in the wrong place or wearing the wrong clothes.
- Prejudice is an idea or feeling which one person holds and which affects another person. This could be when someone prejudges someone else without getting to know them.
- Discrimination is when they act on this prejudice and treat the other person accordingly.
- Discrimination can take place whenever someone with power exercises that power over people who do not have power, so: discrimination = prejudice + power.

Remember

It is important to remember that although laws can be made against discrimination, it is impossible to legislate against what people think; only education may eventually change that.

Key words

Dignity: people should be allowed to live a life in which they have self-respect.
Discrimination: unfair treatment of one person or group.
Equality: treating people in the same way as others.
Fair: something which is free from bias, fraud or injustice. From this meaning it could be said that 'fair' really means 'reasonable'.
Freedom: the concept that everyone in the world should have the freedom to live, think and speak as they want.
Prejudice: the concept that some people prejudge people; they make up their mind about them before they really know them.
Rights: the idea that people have basic requirements which should be respected, e.g. the right to education; the right to be treated with dignity.

Key text

Universal Declaration of Human Rights – the principle of equality is that everyone should be treated fairly without suffering prejudice or discrimination. The principle of equality for everyone is enshrined in the UN Universal Declaration of Human Rights. This statement was signed by the General Assembly of the United Nations (UN) in 1948.

5.2 Biblical teaching about equality

According to Christian teaching God created everything and therefore no one is superior or inferior in God's eyes other than by their own actions.

Main facts

- Jesus taught that people must love others, and that in this way humanity would eventually be saved from war and suffering: 'A new command I give you: Love one another. As I have loved you, so you must love one another' (John 13:34).
- For a Christian, it should make no difference whether people are male or female, black or white, rich or poor. They should all be shown the same love because they are all made in the image of God (Genesis 1:28).
- Biblical teaching about equality is also found in the Acts of the Apostles which explains that God made all people: 'From one man he made every nation of men that they should inhabit the whole earth; and he determined the times set for them and the exact places where they should live' (Acts 17:26).
- Paul also taught that all Christians are equal: 'There is neither Jew nor Greek, slave nor free, male nor female, for you are all one in Christ Jesus' (Galatians 3:28).
- The fight against prejudice and discrimination has been taken up by Christians such as Blessed Mother Teresa who founded the Missionaries of Charity caring for the poor and suffering in India and then across the world. Mother Teresa and her followers lived by the teachings of the Parable of the Sheep and the Goats (Matthew 25:31–46) which says that Christians must care for the poor and the hungry.

Key person

Blessed Mother Teresa (1910–97) – the founder of the Missionaries of Charity in Calcutta, 1950

Remember

As well as creating everything, according to the first creation story in Genesis, God created humans in his own image which shows they are intended to be equal.

Key texts

Matthew 25:31–46 – the Parable of the Sheep and the Goats teaches how people should treat others

John 13:34 – Jesus gave the disciples a new commandment which was to love one another as he had loved them. By showing love to everyone Christians would be treating others fairly

Acts 17:26 – God made everyone, therefore it would be wrong to treat people unfairly because it would be interfering with God's creation

Galatians 3:28–29 – Paul taught that everyone was equal in Christ

5.3 Christian attitudes towards racism

Although Christian teaching has always opposed racism there are many examples in the past of Christians and Christian organisations being guilty of racism.

Main facts

- The biblical teaching on equality shapes Christian attitudes towards racism. Christians are opposed to prejudice and discrimination, including racism.
- One of the main teachings of Jesus against racism is told in the Parable of the Good Samaritan where, in answering the question: 'Who is my neighbour?', Jesus teaches that people should treat everyone well.
- Many Christian denominations and individuals have been and are actively involved in the fight against racism. One famous example is Martin Luther King Jr (1929–68), a Baptist minister who led protests against racial discrimination in the USA in the 1950s and 1960s. He spent most of his life trying to get the law in the USA changed through peaceful protest, and legislation which separated blacks and whites in the USA, called the 'Jim Crow Laws', was finally abolished with the introduction of the Civil Rights Act in 1964.
- However, there have been many occasions over the centuries when the Christian Church has rightly been accused of racism and religious intolerance:
  - During the crusades of the eleventh to thirteenth centuries, thousands of people were killed in the name of Christianity.
  - In South America, during the sixteenth century, the invading Spanish navy massacred tens of thousands of the local people in attempts to force them to become Christians.
  - In what is now the USA, many Christians became very rich slave owners in the 'Deep South'. Slaves were almost always black people. Many of these owners were committed Christians who believed they were helping the slaves by forcing them to convert. However, Christians were very active in the campaigns to end slavery and it was officially abolished after the end of the US Civil War in 1865.
  - In 1948 the South African prime minister, Daniel François Malan, a Dutch Reformed minister, introduced the apartheid legislation into South Africa which segregated black, coloured and white people. Apartheid was not finally abolished until 1994.
- There has been much debate over the silence of the Roman Catholic Church about the persecution of the Jews in Nazi Germany during the Second World War (1939–45).

Key people

Daniel François Malan (1874–1959) – Prime Minister of South Africa from 1948 to 1954

Martin Luther King Jr (1929–68) – a Baptist minister who led protests against racial discrimination in the USA in the 1950s and 1960s. On 4 April 1968 King was assassinated by an escaped white convict, James Earl Ray, in Memphis, Tennessee

Remember

The most famous example of biblical teaching about racism and equality is found in the Parable of the Good Samaritan (Luke 10:26–37).

Key texts

Leviticus 19:33–34 – people should be kind to everyone, including foreigners, because the Israelites themselves had to go to Egypt in times of famine

Luke 10:25–37 – the Parable of the Good Samaritan which teaches that true Christian love is love of everyone no matter who they are or where they come from

Key words

Apartheid: a political system in South Africa from 1948 to the early 1990s that separated the different peoples living there and gave privileges to those of European origin.

Samaritan: somebody who came from ancient Samaria.

5.4 Christian attitudes towards gender and the role of women in Christian society

As Christianity teaches equality, many Christians believe men and women should have equal rights and roles in life. Other Christians believe that men and women have different roles, but that both roles are equally valuable.

Main facts

Some Christians believe men and women should have equal rights and roles. They support this view with teachings such as:

- 'Let us make man in our image' (Genesis 1:26–27) where it says men and women were created at the same time.
- Jesus shows great respect when a woman at Bethany anoints him with oil (Matthew 26:6–13).
- When Jesus rose from the dead he appeared first to Mary Magdalene (Mark 16:9–11).
- In the first days of the early Church, women worshipped together with the disciples (Acts 1:12–14).
- It seems from the writings of Paul that women had greater importance in the early Church (Romans 16:1–5).

However, others think that women and men should have different roles and use teachings such as:

- In Genesis 2 it seems that Adam is made before Eve and she is made as his helper.
- In Genesis 3, it is Eve who is the first to sin.
- Jesus being critical of his mother, Mary, at the wedding at Cana (John 2:3–4a).
- In Paul's first letter to the Corinthians he insists that women must be silent in church and that they should keep their heads covered.
- In recent years an increasing number of Christians have come to feel that women should have an equal role in worship and the priesthood. The Roman Catholic and Orthodox Churches do not agree because they believe the role of the priest is as Jesus' representative on earth and therefore this role cannot be fulfilled by a woman.

Key people

Jesus – treated women as equals against the normal practice of his time
Mary, the mother of Jesus – seen by many Christians as the ideal concept of motherhood because God chose her to be the person to give birth to Jesus
Mary Magdalene – one of the companions of Jesus, showing that he treated women equally
Paul – in his letters, Paul showed contradictory views about women

Remember

It is only in the past 100 years that women have been allowed to be priests or ministers and this is still not permitted in the Roman Catholic and Orthodox Churches.

Key texts

Genesis 1:26–27 – God made humans in his own image showing that everyone is the same
Mark 16:9–11 – at the resurrection Jesus appears first to Mary Magdalene showing that women are important
Acts 1:12–14 – shows the importance of the women in the early Church
Romans 16:1–5 – Paul sends personal greetings to: Phoebe, Priscilla and Mary showing their importance
1 Corinthians 11:3–7; 14:34–35 – Paul teaches that women should cover their heads and be silent when in church showing that men were more important than women

Key words

Lay reader: a lay member of a Church, especially an Anglican Church or the Roman Catholic Church, who is authorised to read some parts of the service. A role which is open to women.
Priest or minister: ordained leader of Christian worship. A role open to women in some denominations but not in the Roman Catholic or Orthodox Churches.

5.5 Christian attitudes towards other religions

Christianity is a proselytising religion. Although Christians believe that everyone should have the right to practise their own religion, they also believe that only Christianity has the complete truth about God. They believe that it is their duty as members of their religion to go out and convert people.

Main facts

- It appears from the New Testament that it is only Jesus' followers who can go to heaven when they die. Jesus taught 'I am the way and the truth and the life' (John 14:6).
- Evangelism is the spreading of the teachings of Jesus from the gospels or 'good news'. This follows Jesus' command to the disciples at his ascension 'Therefore go and make disciples of all nations' (Matthew 28:19a).
- Many Christian groups, such as the Salvation Army, have a strong tradition of evangelism and believe that it is a very important part of their Christian life and duty.
- For centuries, many Christians travelled abroad as missionaries. They believed that it was their Christian duty and obligation to convert as many people to Christianity as possible.
- Missionaries today are now mostly concerned with helping people in developing countries rather than trying to convert them. It could be said that they serve their mission by showing the example of Jesus in their lives.
- Ecumenism is the movement where different Christian denominations work together with joint services and community work. This shows that although there may be major differences between some groups, they still share the same essential beliefs. Taizé, an ecumenical Christian community in a small village in France, was founded in 1940, during the Second World War, by Brother Roger Schutz.
- In recent years, many Christians have started working towards interfaith dialogue, particularly with Jews and Muslims.

Key person

Roger Schutz (1915–2005) – a monk who started the community at Taizé at the end of the Second World War (1939–45) in an attempt to promote reconciliation and break down barriers between denominations

Remember

Today, some Christians believe that evangelising is a misunderstanding of Jesus and that people should follow their own religion and their own God while others believe that they should follow his command to make disciples of all nations.

Key words

Ecumenism: the breaking down of barriers between Christian denominations.
Evangelism: the idea that all Christians should go out into the world to convert people into following Christ.
Missionaries: people who are sent to another country by a Church to spread its faith or to do social and medical work.
Proselytising: to try and convert somebody to a religious faith.

Key text

John 14:6b – 'No one comes to the Father except through me'

5.6 Forgiveness and reconciliation

Forgiveness and reconciliation are very important aspects of Christian life and beliefs. This is demonstrated in, what is for most Christians, the central act of worship, the Eucharist.

Main facts

- A central Christian belief is that of forgiveness as they believe that God is merciful and shows his love and forgiveness of people, and that they should try and show the same attitude. Teachings about forgiveness are found in the Bible. For example:
  - The Lord's Prayer (Matthew 6:9b–13) shows that Christians must always forgive in order to be forgiven by God.
  - Jesus taught his disciples to 'Love your enemies and pray for those who persecute you, that you may be sons of your Father in heaven' (Matthew 5:44–45a). However, this does not mean that Jesus was incapable of anger – that he just forgave everyone anything. He did show his anger when people acted in a way which was offensive to God.
- The central Christian service of the Eucharist is a time for forgiveness and reconciliation when Christians remember and receive God's forgiveness through the celebration of Jesus' sacrifice.
- Jesus gave the power to his disciples to forgive sins on behalf of God, and the Roman Catholic Church teaches that this power has been passed to priests. One of the key beliefs of the Roman Catholic Church is in the sacrament of reconciliation. The person who is seeking forgiveness goes to the priest to ask to be forgiven. The priest hears their confession in a confessional and anything he hears is confidential.
- Jesus taught forgiveness on many occasions including the Parables of the Lost Sheep, Lost Son and the Unforgiving Servant.

Key person

Jesus – his death on the cross was an act of atonement which showed that God had forgiven people for their sins and that if they had truly repented they would be allowed into heaven by God's grace

Remember

There are some places such as Coventry Cathedral, which was rebuilt after being bombed in the Second World War, that have become centres for reconciliation and forgiveness.

Key words

Forgiveness: the act of pardoning or forgiving someone for something which they have done wrong.
Reconciliation: the ending of a conflict or renewing a friendly relationship between disputing people or groups.
Sacrament: an outward, physical sign of an inward, invisible grace.

Key texts

Matthew 6:9b–13 – the Lord's Prayer
John 20:19–23 – Jesus gives the disciples the power of the Holy Spirit to forgive sins

6.1 Different forms of media and their influence

Media can be television, radio, videos, DVDs, CDs, newspapers, magazines, books, posters, advertisements, computers and the internet, social networking sites such as Facebook, art, music, dance and drama. It is anything which is a medium for communicating with other people. There are some religious people who welcome new inventions in the media and communication. There are, however, many others who have mixed feelings about the media and entertainment because of their influence on family life and lifestyles.

Main facts

- When looking at specific issues concerning the media and entertainment, not all Christians share exactly the same opinion. However, Christian ethics are based on two general positive principles that Jesus gave his followers. They are 'love God' and 'love your neighbour'. When Christians are trying to decide what to think and do about an issue, they may turn to various sources of authority to find help:
  - they read the Bible
  - they take the advice of the Church and of their Christian friends
  - they use their conscience and pray to God and ask to be guided by the Holy Spirit.
- Most Christians in the UK do use the media, but they believe that they need to choose carefully what to watch and read. Many Christian families are concerned about the influences that television has on family life. These concerns cover issues of the way in which sex and violence are portrayed and may be seen by children and young people.
- As well as the influence of the media on family life, some Christians are concerned about the influence it has on lifestyles as some of the media present a view of the world that does not fit with Christian views about the priorities in life and the values people should live by. For example, they are worried about how luxury lifestyles portrayed in the media and advertising may have a bad effect, particularly on impressionable young people or older people who are less well educated.
- Many Christians, however, welcome the media because it is a way of spreading the Good News and fulfilling Jesus' commandment at his ascension to 'make disciples of all nations' (Matthew 28:19a). Also, in countries where Christians are persecuted for their beliefs, it allows a way of communication. Some Christians believe that the lifestyles of some celebrity Christians, such as Cliff Richard or Nicky Cruz, are good role models for their children to follow. The Archbishop of Canterbury said that *The Simpsons* was a good role model for family values.

Key words

Conscience: the moral compass within people which some believe is put there by God in order to allow people to do the right actions.
Media: means of mass communication.

Remember

Different groups of Christians may have very different viewpoints about the media dependent on how it is used and whether or not it portrays Christian values.

Key text

Luke 10:25–37 – the Parable of the Good Samaritan includes the Golden Rule of Christianity and may be applied to why Christians approve or disapprove of the media

6.2 The influence of the media on lifestyles

Christianity is not against pleasure but it is against selfishness. Selfish enjoyment is false pleasure according to the Christian viewpoint.

Main facts

- The way the media present the use of alcohol, role models, popular music and astrology is of particular concern to some Christians because of the influence it might have on a person's lifestyle.
- The regular use of alcohol is a feature of many television dramas and in other forms of the media such as magazines. There are different Christian views about alcohol and its influence:
  - Christians belonging to some Protestant evangelical denominations are teetotal; they never drink alcohol. There are individual Christians in other traditions whose conscience may lead them also to abstain from it. They believe that alcohol and the use of drugs can lead people into sin.
  - Other Christians believe that, for themselves, moderation is the key to living in the modern material world. They try to behave responsibly.
  - Christianity is against all forms of addiction because addicts have placed something other than God at the centre of their lives and lifestyles.
- Another way in which the media influence lifestyles is by creating role models. Christians feel that the media tend to make idols of people such as pop and film stars. For some, this is a breaking of the second commandment that tells them not to make idols nor worship false images.
- Popular music has a big influence on young people:
  - Most Christians have no real objection to music and in some countries there is a strong musical tradition associated with Christian worship, for example, hymns or Gospel songs.
  - However, there have always been mixed feelings among Christians towards popular music and the other performing arts, dance and drama. In the present day, most secular popular music continues to be about love and all the sentiments that go with finding love and losing love. Some Christians feel that popular songs trivialise relationships, are too obsessed with sex and may lead to lustful thoughts and bad behaviour.
- Astrology is big business and features in most newspapers. Christians tend to think that basing your life on any sort of fortune telling is silly or wrong and most Christians are uneasy about media themes which they think may lead impressionable people to dabble in the occult.

Key words

Addiction: when people sometimes find it very hard to give up a habit such as smoking, taking drugs or eating chocolate.
Astrology: the idea that people's lives can be predicted from their birth signs.
Moderation: the principle that people should not be excessive in their lives.
Teetotal: not drinking any alcohol.

Remember

Most Christians try to use a principle of moderation in their lives. They are not against people enjoying themselves or enjoying the media, they just think that this should be done wisely.

Key texts

Exodus 20:3–5a – 'do not worship idols', so Christians would believe that worshipping money or people as an idol was wrong
Matthew 5:28–30 – in the Sermon on the Mount Jesus taught that even by thinking lustfully about the opposite sex people are, in fact, committing adultery. Therefore, they should not allow themselves to be tempted into sin
Matthew 16:26 – if people are concerned with material or worldly things all the time they will damage their soul

6.3 The way Christianity uses the media

Christianity has no united policy about the media or its use. However, all Christians would be opposed to misuse of the media if it is seen to disregard Christian values.

Main facts

- Some Christian sects such as the Amish, Mennonites and Exclusive Plymouth Brethren do not approve of almost any type of secular entertainment. However, the Amish have paid for a website to be created so that other people can find out about their beliefs without troubling them.
- There are many ways in which Christians use the media to present a positive and accurate representation of their religion. This may include television programmes such as *Songs of Praise*.
- Evangelical Churches often use drama, dance and art, especially when leading campaigns for young people. They believe that Christianity is exciting so feel that they should use appropriate media to convey this message.
- Comics for children which retell stories from the Bible or the lives of famous Christians are also seen as a way of spreading the message of Christianity in a way that makes most sense to young people.
- Television programmes such as *Songs of Praise* help to bring Christianity into the lives of people who might not go to church. There are also several evangelical 'God' channels now available.
- Christians may use the media to educate others, such as the websites of the Church of England and the Vatican.

Key words

Evangelical: Christians who stress the authority of the Bible and salvation through personal acceptance of Jesus.
Secular: non-religious ideas.

Remember

Many Churches use big musical events to celebrate their beliefs with a wider community. An example of where music is used to portray Christian beliefs is the annual Greenbelt festival which began in 1974 and celebrates arts, faith and justice. They believe that in the modern world Christianity needs to engage with people on their terms, so that people can see that Christianity is relevant to them and their lives.

6.4 How important religious figures and Christianity are portrayed in the media

Christians are divided over the media but a common concern is that the media should not lead people to worship false gods or idols.

Main facts

- Religious people sometimes feel uncomfortable at the representation of important religious figures in drama. For example, some Christians think that God or Jesus should not be acted by a human being because ordinary people are not perfect like God.
- Some Christians are not only against the representation of important religious people but also of any person and all living creatures. This view is based on the first two commandments given by God to the prophet Moses:
  - The first commandment is about not having other gods besides the one God.
  - The second commandment says: 'You shall not make for yourself an idol in the form of anything in heaven above or on the earth beneath or in the waters below. You shall not bow down to them or worship them …' (Exodus 20:4–5a).
- One result of this belief was seen in England during the civil war (1642–51): the Roundheads and Puritans smashed stained-glass windows because they wanted to cleanse the churches of idolatrous images. Even today many denominations within the Christian Church believe that these images would cause distractions to worship.
- Often the portrayal of important religious figures in the media is negative. The Archbishop of Canterbury and Pope Benedict XVI are usually only in the news if they have put forward a controversial view; whereas Pope John Paul II was often portrayed in a more positive light.
- There are now many Christian websites which are used as a way of preaching the message of Jesus to both Christians and non-Christians.

> **Remember**
>
> Many Christians see the media as useful because it can help them spread their message and fulfil Jesus' command to 'go and make disciples of all nations' (Matthew 28:18a).

> **Key text**
>
> **Exodus 20:3–5a** – 'do not worship idols', so Christians would believe that worshipping money or people as an idol was wrong

> **Key word**
>
> Idolatry: the worship of idols or false gods.

6.5 Christian responses and attitudes towards films and other media which focus on religious/philosophical messages

Some Christians have always felt important religious figures should not be represented in the media. However, in recent years, some films portraying Jesus have been approved of by the Church.

Main facts

- At first, many Christians were shocked when rock musicals on biblical themes such as *Godspell*, *Jesus Christ Superstar* and *Joseph* were performed, but most Christians and Churches who are not against using the media have now accepted these musicals and watch them on television or on the stage. This suggests that some attitudes have changed over the past fifty years.

- Books, plays and films have used themes from Christian teachings and in some the use of sex and violence, or humour, has appalled some Christians. One example is *Monty Python's Life of Brian*. Some Christians believe that anything which does not show respect when dealing with Christianity is wrong. Other Christians might say 'this is just a story'. The film *Bruce Almighty* caused Christians to disagree: some said it was wrong because it showed God 'giving away his powers', while others believed that the Golden Rule of Christianity was demonstrated through humour.

- In recent years there have been many popular books about Christianity and the Church. Perhaps the best known is *The Da Vinci Code* by Dan Brown, published in 2003. The book, and the film of it which followed in 2006, made millions of people think more about Christianity and the Church, but many Christians objected to it because it suggests that Jesus married Mary Magdalene and had a child and many Christians believe this is untrue.

Remember

Many Christians think that, rather than it being wrong to make films or musicals about Jesus and other biblical characters, these may serve to bring the message of Christianity to many people who would otherwise not know about it.

Key text

Exodus 20:3–5a – 'do not worship idols', so Christians would believe that worshipping money or people as an idol was wrong

6.6 Christian beliefs and attitudes towards the portrayal of sex and violence

There is no unified Christian opinion about the portrayal of sex and violence in the media but there is a common concern that these should not become a bad influence on people.

Main facts

- Many Christians are concerned about the amount of violence and sex in the media because they believe it can lead people into believing that violence and casual sex is not wrong. For example, soap operas such as *EastEnders* often show extramarital relationships in such a way as to suggest that everyone accepts these as right.
- Christians might criticise the media about particular violent films such as *Pulp Fiction* and may decide to boycott them. Indeed, some Christians thought that Mel Gibson's film *The Passion of the Christ* was too violent in its portrayal of the flogging and the crucifixion.
- Therefore, some people feel that the media encourage violence while others disagree, but there is another important issue. People may no longer be shocked by the physical or verbal abuse of vulnerable members of society. It may be that, as a result, more people become victims of violence, particularly women and children, and the public does less and less about it.
- The rising numbers of cases of rape, murder and sexual abuse of women and children which are reported are often blamed on the media and it is claimed that people copy what they see.
- Many Christian Churches are likely to condemn the media for any material which seems to condone promiscuity, premarital sex, adultery and homosexuality.
- Christians believe pornography is wrong because they think it exploits people as sex objects. Although pornography is wrong in the opinion of some people, not only Christians, changing social attitudes now mean that it is no longer a criminal offence in most Western countries.

Remember

Many people, including Christians, blame the media for a moral decay in society. However, there is very little evidence for this.

Key texts

1 Corinthians 13:4–8 – Paul states that love is the most important quality to have and Christians interpret this to show that the values portrayed in the media are often wrong

Philippians 4:8 – this gives the qualities which are praiseworthy such as love and truth, showing that these qualities should be the focus of a Christian life rather than the ones portrayed in the media

Key word

Pornography: the explicit description or showing of sexual activity to stimulate sexual excitement.

6.7 Censorship and freedom of speech

Freedom of speech is the right of people to say what they think without censorship. It is important to Christians although they may still object to offensive remarks about their own religion.

Main facts

- Freedom of speech and freedom of the press are important means of making sure that countries do not become dictatorships or police states. However, there are many countries which do not permit these freedoms and even those which do, such as the UK, still place some limitations on what can be said or published.
- One of the reasons that people in the Western world are suspicious of censorship is because it is a method of control and suppression which has been used by totalitarian states such as Nazi Germany and the Soviet Union in the past.
- The most dramatic censorship of written material is perhaps when books are burnt. Burning books has become a symbol of a society trying to control the people. In 1933, the Nazis burnt books which held 'un-German' ideas.
- One of the important issues concerning censorship in the UK has been the laws against blasphemy.
- In the 1980s, when Salman Rushdie wrote *The Satanic Verses* which caused offence to many Muslims, the courts decided that, in England, blasphemy only offered protection to Christianity and possibly only to the Church of England.
- Until 2008 when the law was repealed, blasphemy was a criminal offence.
- In the UK and Europe people are free to express their views about any religion unless the content is likely to incite violence or discrimination against its followers.
- However, in some countries, such as North Korea, Christians are not allowed to proclaim their beliefs.

Remember

When thinking about Christian views on issues of censorship, it is important to distinguish between crimes and sins. Crimes break the laws of the state. Sins break commands which people believe came from God. Some actions, like murder, are both a sin and a crime.

The term 'Big Brother is watching you' was first used in the book *Nineteen Eighty-Four* by George Orwell. It was published in 1949 but it was set in a fictional nightmare future where there was total invasion of privacy and no freedom of speech.

Key words

Blasphemy: the act of showing disrespect for God.
Censorship: controlling or stopping something being published or said by the media.
Freedom of speech: the belief that no-one should be punished for what they say.
Propaganda: information put out by an organisation or government to persuade people to think in the same way as them.

On pages 79–82 are exam-style questions for each topic. Outlines to help you answer or to check your answer are provided on pages 83–94.

Unit B601 Philosophy 1

Topic 1 Beliefs about deity

(a) Name one way in which Christians believe God intervenes in the world. *(1 mark)*

(b) What is a miracle? *(2 marks)*

(c) Describe three things which Christians believe about Jesus. *(3 marks)*

(d) Explain some of the reasons which people give to support their belief in God. *(6 marks)*

(e) 'If God existed we would know.'

Discuss this statement. You should include different, supported points of view and a personal viewpoint. You must refer to Christianity in your answer. *(12 marks)*

Topic 2 Religious and spiritual experience

(a) Name one Christian prayer. *(1 mark)*

(b) What is meant by fasting? *(2 marks)*

(c) Describe the use of Christian symbols in worship. *(3 marks)*

(d) Explain how some Christians use music to express their belief in God. *(6 marks)*

(e) 'Money should be given to the poor, not spent on places of worship.'

Discuss this statement. You should include different, supported points of view and a personal viewpoint. You must refer to Christianity in your answer. *(12 marks)*

Topic 3 The end of life

(a) What is the soul? *(1 mark)*

(b) Name two things Christians believe about heaven. *(2 marks)*

(c) Describe what some Christians believe about purgatory. *(3 marks)*

(d) Explain why the suffering of Christ is important for Christians. *(6 marks)*

(e) 'Funerals are for the living, not the dead.'

Discuss this statement. You should include different, supported points of view and a personal viewpoint. You must refer to Christianity in your answer. *(12 marks)*

Unit B601 Philosophy 2

Topic 4 Good and evil

(a) What is meant by 'evil'? *(1 mark)*

(b) Name two things Christians believe about the Devil (Satan). *(2 marks)*

(c) Describe what is meant by 'original sin'. *(3 marks)*

(d) Explain how some Christians may respond to suffering in the world. *(6 marks)*

(e) 'If people want to know how to behave they should just read the Bible.'

Discuss this statement. You should include different, supported points of view and a personal viewpoint. You must refer to Christianity in your answer. *(12 marks)*

Topic 5 Religion, reason and revelation

(a) What is meant by 'revelation'? *(1 mark)*

(b) Give two examples of mystical experiences. *(2 marks)*

(c) Describe what is in the Bible. *(3 marks)*

(d) Explain how Christians believe that God can be revealed through the world. *(6 marks)*

(e) 'The Bible is too old to have any real importance today.'

Discuss this statement. You should include different, supported points of view and a personal viewpoint. You must refer to Christianity in your answer. *(12 marks)*

Topic 6 Religion and science

(a) How many creation stories are there in the book of Genesis? *(1 mark)*

(b) What is meant by stewardship? *(2 marks)*

(c) Give three examples of environmental issues which might concern Christians. *(3 marks)*

(d) Explain why some Christians might find it difficult to accept the story of creation. *(6 marks)*

(e) 'Religious people have a special duty to care for the environment.'

Discuss this statement. You should include different, supported points of view and a personal viewpoint. You must refer to Christianity in your answer. *(12 marks)*

Unit B603 Applied Ethics 1

Topic 1 Religion and human relationships

(a) What is contraception? *(1 mark)*

(b) Give two reasons why Christian might think the use of contraception is wrong. *(2 marks)*

(c) Describe Christian attitudes towards civil partnerships. *(3 marks)*

(d) Explain why some Christians are opposed to divorce. *(6 marks)*

(e) 'Marriage is out of date, people should just live together.'

Discuss this statement. You should include different, supported points of view and a personal viewpoint. You must refer to Christianity in your answer. *(12 marks)*

Topic 2 Religions and medical ethics

(a) What is cloning? *(1 mark)*

(b) What is meant by euthanasia? *(2 marks)*

(c) What are Christian attitudes towards suicide? *(3 marks)*

(d) Explain why many Christians are opposed to abortion. *(6 marks)*

(e) 'Animals should be used in medical research as they are not as important as humans.'

Discuss this statement. You should include different, supported points of view and a personal viewpoint. You must refer to Christianity in your answer. *(12 marks)*

Topic 3 Religion, poverty and wealth

(a) Give an example of what a Christian would consider a moral occupation. *(1 mark)*

(b) Give two examples of what Christians might consider immoral occupations. *(2 marks)*

(c) What does the Bible teach about caring for others? *(3 marks)*

(d) Explain different ways in which Christians might put charity into practice. *(6 marks)*

(e) 'Religious people should always help others who are suffering.'

Discuss this statement. You should include different, supported points of view and a personal viewpoint. You must refer to Christianity in your answer. *(12 marks)*

Unit B604 Applied Ethics 2

Topic 4 Religion, peace and justice

(a) What is capital punishment? *(1 mark)*

(b) Give two of the conditions for a 'just war'. *(2 marks)*

(c) Describe Christian views on the aims of punishment. *(3 marks)*

(d) Explain how Christians might respond to social injustice. *(6 marks)*

(e) 'Criminals should be punished, not forgiven.'

Discuss this statement. You should include different, supported points of view and a personal viewpoint. You must refer to Christianity in your answer. *(12 marks)*

Topic 5 Religion and equality

(a) What is meant by 'prejudice'? *(1 mark)*

(b) Give two examples of discrimination. *(2 marks)*

(c) Describe how some Christians are working towards ecumenism. *(3 marks)*

(d) Explain Christian teaching about the role of women in the Church. *(6 marks)*

(e) 'All people must be treated equally.'

Discuss this statement. You should include different, supported points of view and a personal viewpoint. You must refer to Christianity in your answer. *(12 marks)*

Topic 6 Religion and the media

(a) Give one example of the media. *(1 mark)*

(b) What does 'censorship' mean? *(2 marks)*

(c) Describe how Christians might use the media. *(3 marks)*

(d) Explain Christian attitudes towards the portrayal of sex in the media. *(6 marks)*

(e) 'Important religious figures such as Jesus should not be portrayed in the media.'

Discuss this statement. You should include different, supported points of view and a personal viewpoint. You must refer to Christianity in your answer. *(12 marks)*

Topic 1 Beliefs about deity

These answers provide an outline of how you could construct your response. For the higher mark answers you should add your own specific examples and Bible teachings, which should be explained to show your understanding (see pages 3–4 for more guidance on this).

(a) Name one way in which Christians believe God intervenes in the world. *(1 mark)*

Christians believe God intervenes in the world through miracles.

(b) What is a miracle? *(2 marks)*

A miracle is an event that appears to be against the laws of nature and is regarded as an act of God.

(c) Describe three things which Christians believe about Jesus. *(3 marks)*

Christians believe that Jesus was the Son of God and part of the Trinity. They also believe that Jesus' mother Mary was a virgin which shows the miracle of Jesus' birth. They believe that Jesus died on the cross and then rose from the dead.

(d) Explain some of the reasons which people give to support their belief in God. *(6 marks)*

There are many reasons which people might give to support their belief in God. They might use one of the arguments for the existence of God. They might say that the universe is so complex that it must have had a designer, or that something must have started all life and that this was God. Some people might believe in God because they have had a religious experience such as hearing God speak to them. Other people might say that they believe in God because they believe what is written in the Bible because this is the truth about God.

(e) 'If God existed we would know.' Discuss this statement. You should include different, supported points of view and a personal viewpoint. You must refer to Christianity in your answer. *(12 marks)*

Some Christians might say that they do know that God exists. They might explain that God performs miracles and answers prayers. They might also say that they can see God by looking around them at the world and all the forms of life in it. Christians might say that for them the Bible proves that God exists and that they are aware of God's influence in their own lives.

Many people who do not believe in God would probably agree with the statement. They would say that there is no evidence at all to show that God exists and that this suggests that there is no God. However, some people might say that there could be a God but it is just that God chooses not to be seen or experienced by humans, in which case there is no proof either way.

As I am a Christian I believe that God does exist and I think that I have experienced God sometimes when I go to church and also when I pray at home. One of my Christian friends believes that God exists simply because she has faith.

Examiner's comments:
These are all very good answers. The first three, which are all knowledge answers, give specific facts in answer to the questions. The answer to (d) shows a wide variety of different reasons for belief. It also explains these reasons through the use of the word 'because'. The answer to (e) also shows a variety of opinions including Christian ones, different non-Christian views and also a personal response.

Topic 2 Religious and spiritual experience

These answers provide an outline of how you could construct your response. For the higher mark answers you should add your own specific examples and Bible teachings, which should be explained to show your understanding (see pages 3–4 for more guidance on this).

(a) Name one Christian prayer. *(1 mark)*

One Christian prayer is the Lord's Prayer.

(b) What is meant by fasting? *(2 marks)*

Fasting is when people choose not to eat for a period of time, usually for religious reasons.

(c) Describe the use of Christian symbols in worship. *(3 marks)*

There are many symbols which some Christians use in their worship. They may use a cross or a crucifix to remind them of when Jesus was crucified. A lit candle may remind them that Jesus is called the 'Light of the World'. In the Eucharist Christians take wine and bread which symbolise the blood and body of Christ.

(d) Explain how some Christians use music to express their belief in God. *(6 marks)*

Although some Christians such as members of the Religious Society of Friends (Quakers) do not use music in their worship because they worship in silence waiting for the power of the Holy Spirit most Christians do. This music may be very formal and led by a choir. This may include psalms from the Bible or hymns and the congregation may also join in. This shows their belief in God because the psalms were written by people inspired by God and the psalms and hymns show what they believe about God; such as Psalm 23 'The Lord is my Shepherd'. Other Christians use more informal music such as Gospel singing in order to show their enthusiasm and love for God because they believe God loves them; he is omnibenevolent.

(e) 'Money should be given to the poor, not spent on places of worship.'
Discuss this statement. You should include different, supported points of view and a personal viewpoint. You must refer to Christianity in your answer. *(12 marks)*

All Christians have a duty to care for the poor and try to help them and so some people might agree with this statement completely. They might say that all Christians should live their lives like Jesus and his disciples who did not have many possessions. However, many other Christians, while they would agree about caring for the poor, would also say that a place of worship is God's house and that therefore, out of love and respect, they should make it as beautiful as possible. People might also feel that a beautiful place of worship helps people focus their thoughts on God when they are there. The argument about whether or not to spend money making a place of worship beautiful still continues especially when some cathedrals need a lot of money for their upkeep and yet there is so much poverty in the world.

People who do not believe in God would probably say that caring for the poor is a human duty and that money spent on places of worship is simply wasted.

In my opinion, as I am an atheist, I think that it is far more important to give charity and care for the poor because what is the point of spending money on a place of worship for something that does not exist?

> **Examiner's comments:**
> Each of these responses is good and gains full marks. The first three, which are all knowledge answers, give specific facts in answer to the questions. The answer to (d) shows a range of ideas of the use of music. It also explains these ideas which is shown through the use of the word 'because', while the response to (e) shows different Christian views as well as a humanitarian position and a personal response.

Topic 3 The end of life

These answers provide an outline of how you could construct your response. For the higher mark answers you should add your own specific examples and Bible teachings, which should be explained to show your understanding (see pages 3–4 for more guidance on this).

(a) What is the soul? *(1 mark)*

The part of a human being which is separate from the body and which Christians believe will go to heaven.

(b) Name two things Christians believe about heaven. *(2 marks)*

Christians believe that heaven is a place where they may go after death if they have lived a good life. They also believe that it is being with God permanently.

(c) Describe what some Christians believe about purgatory. *(3 marks)*

Some Christians, particularly Roman Catholics, believe that there are very few people whose lives have been so good that they will go straight to heaven when they die. They believe that most people will go to purgatory where they will be cleansed of their sins and be made ready for heaven. At the funeral, Catholics will say prayers to ask God to release the person from purgatory as soon as possible.

(d) Explain why the suffering of Christ is important for Christians. *(6 marks)*

Christ suffered at the hands of the Romans and was then nailed to the cross where he lived for three hours before dying. This suffering is very important for Christians because they believe that Jesus was the Son of God and was carrying out God's plan to atone for the sins of the world. His suffering is also important because he voluntarily chose to die in this way for the sins of humanity so that people would then have the opportunity to go to heaven. Christians see this suffering as the great love which God has for people and also believe that because Christ suffered they should be prepared to suffer as well, such as Mother Teresa refusing painkillers when she was dying.

(e) 'Funerals are for the living, not the dead.' Discuss this statement. You should include different, supported points of view and a personal viewpoint. You must refer to Christianity in your answer. *(12 marks)*

Some Christians might say that this statement is obvious because the dead people are not able to experience the funeral, therefore its main purpose is to offer comfort to the living and give them a chance to finally say goodbye to the person who has died. These people may say that the funeral service is designed to remind people of their Christian beliefs and the hope that they are now with Jesus in heaven.

Other Christians believe that the funeral service is a necessary part of the person going to heaven and that the prayers which are said asking God to take care of their loved ones help people into heaven.

Non-believers would see funerals as simply a mark of respect for the person who has died.

I am a Catholic and I believe that the prayers which we say at funerals are important to help ensure that people spend as little time as possible in purgatory and are soon united with God.

Examiner's comments:
All parts of this question are well answered. Part (c) has a good explanation of the idea of purgatory. Part (d) is a difficult question but this is a good explanation of the importance of Jesus' suffering and the ideas are explained, using the word 'because'. Finally, part (e) shows a breadth of Christian opinions as well as a secular view and a supported personal response.

Topic 4 Good and evil

These answers provide an outline of how you could construct your response. For the higher mark answers you should add your own specific examples and Bible teachings, which should be explained to show your understanding (see pages 3–4 for more guidance on this).

(a) What is meant by 'evil'? *(1 mark)*

Evil is something which is wrong or immoral.

(b) Name two things Christians believe about the Devil (Satan). *(2 marks)*

Many Christians believe that the Devil is a fallen angel (Lucifer). They believe that he tries to persuade people to do evil rather than good.

(c) Describe what is meant by 'original sin'. *(3 marks)*

'Original sin' is the term used to explain how when God created the world everything was good, yet there is evil present in the world today. Christians believe that when Eve picked the fruit from the tree of the Knowledge of Good and Evil in the Garden of Eden and ate it this introduced original sin into the world. Since then everyone is born with original sin which is cleansed at baptism.

(d) Explain how some Christians may respond to suffering in the world. *(6 marks)*

Most Christians would probably respond to suffering in the world by trying to do something to help bring it to an end or to help the people who are suffering. They would do this because they want to follow Jesus' example and teaching about agape and loving your neighbour. This may involve giving money or working to raise money for charities which help people who are suffering or it may be more practical. They may decide to give their time and travel to places where people are suffering for whatever reason and try to help them directly because they know that they will be judged on their deeds and thoughts when they die. Christians might also pray to ask God to help these people because they know from the teachings of Jesus that God answers prayers.

(e) 'If people want to know how to behave they should just read the Bible.'
Discuss this statement. You should include different, supported points of view and a personal viewpoint. You must refer to Christianity in your answer. *(12 marks)*

Many Christians might agree with this statement, saying that everything they need to know about how God wants them to live can be found in the Bible which is the Word of God. Others may feel that they need to think carefully about how to behave in certain situations. Therefore, they might pray and ask God to give them guidance or perhaps ask a minister, a priest or a Christian friend for advice about what to do. They may also consider the teaching of the Church about how they should respond to a situation. An example would be whether or not to tell someone in authority if they saw someone stealing from another person. The Christian would think about the commandment 'do not steal' and also ask their conscience what would be the best thing to do.

Non-Christians would probably not turn to the Bible as a source of advice. They are more likely to really on their own conscience and the advice of other people that they respect in order to make decisions about how they should behave in a particular situation.

As I am a Christian I ask myself 'what would Jesus do?' when confronted by a difficult decision. For instance if I saw someone being bullied I would know Jesus would want me to help that person because I would be following his teaching of 'love your neighbour'.

> **Examiner's comments:**
> Part (c) gives a good description of the idea of original sin. Part (d) is a well-focused response which suggests ways in which different Christians might respond to suffering in the world and explains the ideas. Part (e) is well-argued and gives a range of Christian and secular views as well as a personal response. An example is also given to show the examiner their full understanding of the question.

Topic 5 Religion, reason and revelation

These answers provide an outline of how you could construct your response. For the higher mark answers you should add your own specific examples and Bible teachings, which should be explained to show your understanding (see pages 3–4 for more guidance on this).

(a) What is meant by 'revelation'? *(1 mark)*

When Christians use the word 'revelation' they mean teachings which come from God.

(b) Give two examples of mystical experiences. *(2 marks)*

Two well-known examples of mystical experiences which are direct experiences of a religious nature are the appearance of the Virgin Mary to Bernadette Soubirous at Lourdes in France and when the Virgin Mary, St Joseph and St John the Evangelist appeared to people at Knock Parish Church in Ireland.

(c) Describe what is in the Bible. *(3 marks)*

The Bible contains many different types of writing. It is in two parts, the Old Testament which is the Jewish scriptures and the New Testament which is about the life and teachings of Jesus and the early Church. The Old Testament contains law, history, prophecy and poetry. In the New Testament are the gospels and letters to the first Christians from Paul and other Apostles.

(d) Explain how Christians believe that God can be revealed through the world. *(6 marks)*

Christians believe that God can be revealed through the world in many ways: such as design, beauty, the conscience and miracles. Some Christians might use the design argument and say that the complexity of the world and the universe shows that there must be a creator and that this is how God is revealed. Others might say that by simply looking around the world there is so much variety in landscape, plants and animals and so much beauty to see that this must be God's work and therefore he is revealed in this way. Some might say that the fact that humans have an in-built sense of right and wrong such as the conscience is evidence that there is a God who places that in us. This is called general or natural revelation. Others believe that when a miracle happens, such as someone being cured, this is God revealing his love and all-powerfulness.

(e) 'The Bible is too old to have any real importance today.'
Discuss this statement. You should include different, supported points of view and a personal viewpoint. You must refer to Christianity in your answer. *(12 marks)*

It is very easy to agree with this statement if you are not a Christian because you might say that it has never had any real importance anyway. On the other hand, some non-Christians might say that, even though they do not believe that the Bible comes from God, nevertheless it does contain important ideas about how people should treat each other, such as the Ten Commandments which contain rules for society: do not murder, etc. Even so, many would agree that the Bible was not designed for this modern technological world because, for instance, there are no specific teachings on fertility treatment or cloning.

Christians would disagree with this statement. Although different groups of Christians regard the Bible in different ways, nevertheless they see it as a special revelation from God. Some Christians believe that the Bible is the actual Word of God and that everything in it therefore must be true and factual and that they should live their lives according to what it teaches. Others may believe that it is the work of humans, inspired by God, and that therefore it needs to be interpreted for today. However, they would probably all agree with the fact that even though the Bible is so old, it is still used by Christians today: this, therefore, proves its importance.

Although I am a Christian and I do read the Bible sometimes, I think that a lot of it is difficult to understand and therefore it needs to be explained to people, which is what the vicar tries to do in the sermon and Bible classes.

Examiner's comments:
All the responses are very good. In (b) there are two good examples of mystical experiences, (c) explains some of the different types of writing found in the Bible, (d) is a full explanation of general revelation with different ideas about this and (e) is a good analysis of special revelation with a consideration of different Christian and non-Christian views.

Topic 6 Religion and science

These answers provide an outline of how you could construct your response. For the higher mark answers you should add your own specific examples and Bible teachings, which should be explained to show your understanding (see pages 3–4 for more guidance on this).

(a) How many creation stories are there in the book of Genesis? *(1 mark)*

There are two creation stories.

(b What is meant by stewardship? *(2 marks)*

Stewardship means looking after something for someone else, such as Christians believe they should be looking after the world for God.

(c) Give three examples of environmental issues which might concern Christians. *(3 marks)*

Pollution such as litter, the destruction of the ozone layer through the misuse of CFCs and the loss of natural habitats for animals and plants through deforestation might all concern Christians because they believe God wants them to be stewards of the earth.

(d) Explain why some Christians might find it difficult to accept the story of creation. *(6 marks)*

Many Christians might find it difficult to accept the Creation stories in Genesis because they seem to be contradicted by modern scientific discoveries. Science has shown that the universe was almost certainly created by an explosion called the 'Big Bang' but some Christians believe God created it by command 'let there be'. As well as this, Darwin's theory of evolution shows that life forms change and develop over time whereas some Christians feel that God created humans in 'his image'. Other Christians might consider that the creation stories are myths which are designed to explain that God was responsible for the whole of creation but are not supposed to be taken as literal truth.

Christians who take the Bible very literally might say that science is wrong.

(e) 'Religious people have a special duty to care for the environment.'
Discuss this statement. You should include different, supported points of view and a personal viewpoint. You must refer to Christianity in your answer. *(12 marks)*

Most Christians believe that God gave them a special responsibility of stewardship because God put Adam in the Garden of Eden to care for it and that therefore it is their responsibility to take care of the earth and all the life which is on it. They believe that this is a duty which God has given them because there are many teachings in the Bible which say so, such as the story of Noah, and also that they need to ensure that the earth remains a place where future generations can live.

A non-religious person might think that the earth should be left to take care of itself. However, many non-religious people would take exactly the same attitude as Christians and believe that everyone has a duty to future generations to ensure that the earth survives.

I am not a Christian but I think that caring for the earth and all the life on it is one of the most important responsibilities for all people whether they are religious or not and if it is not looked after then there are going to be disastrous effects such as climate change.

Examiner's comments:
The answer to (d) is very good because it explains the conflict which some Christians find between the creation stories and scientific discoveries. It also explains the concept of myth well. In (e) there are a good range of opinions with supporting argument and a personal opinion is included.

Topic 1 Religion and human relationships

These answers provide an outline of how you could construct your response. For the higher mark answers you should add your own specific examples and Bible teachings, which should be explained to show your understanding (see pages 3–4 for more guidance on this).

(a) What is contraception? *(1 mark)*

Contraception is something which is intended to prevent a woman becoming pregnant.

(b) Give two reasons why Christians might think the use of contraception is wrong. *(2 marks)*

Christians might believe that artificial contraception is wrong because God told people to 'go forth and multiply'. They might also think that sex should not be used simply for pleasure and that there should be a chance of a baby being conceived.

(c) Describe Christian attitudes towards civil partnerships. *(3 marks)*

Christians have different attitudes towards civil partnerships. Some believe that all homosexual acts are sinful and therefore people of the same sex should not be in a relationship like this. Others think that civil partnerships are a good way for homosexual couples to show their love and commitment. Others may think because a civil partnership is not a religious ceremony then they do not matter.

(d) Explain why some Christians are opposed to divorce. *(6 marks)*

Many Christians and, in particular, Roman Catholics, believe that marriage is a sacrament and that the promises made before God are binding until one of the parties dies. A sacrament cannot be undone and therefore these Christians are opposed to divorce in all circumstances. In certain cases the Roman Catholic Church may decide that the marriage was not valid and therefore not a sacrament and allow the couple to have an annulment. This means that they are then free to marry someone else in the church.

Jesus' teachings about divorce are found in the Sermon on the Mount and in Mark's gospel. Jesus appeared to be opposed to divorce because he said God had created man and woman to be 'one flesh' and therefore they should not be separated.

However, some Christians, although they do not welcome divorce, still feel that in some cases it can be the lesser of two evils.

(e) 'Marriage is out of date, people should just live together.'
Discuss this statement. You should include different, supported points of view and a personal viewpoint. You must refer to Christianity in your answer. *(12 marks)*

Some liberal Christians, while not agreeing with this statement, might say that it is better if people live together before they are married to see how they get on. However, most Christians would not agree that marriage is out of date. They consider that marriage is the only way in which men and women should live together and have sex with each other. They believe that marriage was set up by God and its importance was stressed by Jesus when he attended the wedding at Cana and also in his teaching. Most Christians believe that, whenever possible, children should be brought up in a family with a mother and father who are married to each other. They believe that marriage is a sacrament which means the relationship is blessed by God.

Many non-religious people might agree with the statement. They might think that marriage is an old-fashioned religious idea which ties people together and too often ends in divorce. However, there are non-religious people who feel that a civil marriage ceremony is a good thing because it offers some legal protection to the couple and also reflects their wishes to be committed to each other. Also, some non-religious people want a church wedding just because they like the ceremony and tradition of them.

My parents are divorced and I sometimes think that they would have been better off if they had not married each other. However, I still feel that in the future I would like to be married myself in order to show that I am serious about a relationship.

Examiner's comments:
This is an excellent response to the question. In each part the candidate has given a very full answer and in (c), (d) and (e) has included a range of views. In (e) in particular there is good argument with thoughtful reflection.

Topic 2 Religion and medical ethics

These answers provide an outline of how you could construct your response. For the higher mark answers you should add your own specific examples and Bible teachings, which should be explained to show your understanding (see pages 3–4 for more guidance on this).

(a) What is cloning? *(1 mark)*

Cloning is the technique of making an exact copy of a plant or animal.

(b) What is meant by euthanasia? *(2 marks)*

The term 'euthanasia' is explained by the statement: an easy or gentle death. It is when someone helps someone who is suffering from a terminal disease to die with dignity and as least pain as possible.

(c) What are Christian attitudes towards suicide? *(3 marks)*

Some Christians think that suicide is a sin because they believe that only God has the right to decide when a life should end because he is the one who gives and takes life as stated by Job in the Old Testament. Although the Roman Catholic Church believes that suicide is wrong, it does not think that anyone who was thinking properly would choose to end their life, and so it is regarded as the unfortunate outcome of a mental condition. Some other Christians believe that someone who is suffering should show their trust in God and not commit suicide.

(d) Explain why many Christians are opposed to abortion. *(6 marks)*

Many Christians, particularly Roman Catholics, believe that God chooses when a woman becomes pregnant and that life begins at conception. A procured abortion (not a miscarriage) is therefore seen as murder which is against the sixth commandment because a life is being ended. The only circumstances under which Roman Catholics will accept an abortion is when it is the result of a necessary treatment. For example, if a woman has an ectopic pregnancy this must be ended to save her life. The baby will die as a result but it would not survive anyway. This is called the 'doctrine of double effect'.

Some other Christians accept that in certain circumstances abortion may be the right choice, such as when the mother is too young or the child is the result of rape, because of the concept of agape. However, an abortion is never welcomed.

(e) 'Animals should be used in medical research as they are not as important as humans.' Discuss this statement. You should include different, supported points of view and a personal viewpoint. You must refer to Christianity in your answer. *(12 marks)*

Most Christians do not believe that animals have souls. They believe that this is what makes animals different from humans. They also believe that humankind was given dominion over the animals as was shown when Adam named them. Some people might say that therefore animals are not as important as humans and should be used for medical research which can help humans. They would probably be opposed to the use of animals for cosmetic testing however.

On the other hand many Christians would not really accept this view and would think that animals should be treated with equal respect and that they should not be used for research. The Quakers believe this because they see animals and humans as being as important as each other because they are all God's creation.

Non-religious people do not believe that animals have souls but many of them would still be opposed to the use of animals for medical research because it is seen to be cruel.

I am not sure whether animals have souls or not but I think that we must accept that sometimes, when a new treatment for a serious disease is too dangerous to test on humans, it may be necessary to use animals provided that everything possible is done to keep any pain to the minimum.

Examiner's comments:
These are all very good and thorough responses showing a wide range of views and opinions supported by biblical references. Part (e) is well argued with good, supported views and an interesting personal response.

Topic 3 Religion, poverty and wealth

These answers provide an outline of how you could construct your response. For the higher mark answers you should add your own specific examples and Bible teachings, which should be explained to show your understanding (see pages 3–4 for more guidance on this).

(a) Give an example of what a Christian would consider a moral occupation. *(1 mark)*

Most Christians would consider being a nurse or doctor a moral occupation.

(b) Give two examples of what Christians might consider immoral occupations. *(2 marks)*

Most Christians would consider drug dealing and prostitution to be immoral occupations because they harm people.

(c) What does the Bible teach about caring for others? *(3 marks)*

In the Old Testament it says that strangers should be treated as well as your own family. In the New Testament Jesus says that the second most important Commandment is to love your neighbour as yourself. In the parable of the Sheep and the Goats, Jesus taught that if people do not care for the poor and unwanted then they will be judged on Judgement Day and sent to hell.

(d) Explain different ways in which Christians might put charity into practice. *(6 marks)*

The New Testament has many teachings about charity, love, giving and concern for others. Some Christians may put this into practice by giving regularly to one or more charities, such as CAFOD, which work to help other people with either short-term aid (disasters), or long-term aid (helping people to be self-sufficient) because this is a way of showing agape and following the teachings in the parable of the sheep and goats. Some people might think that they should give their time and their energies to help other people through a charitable organisation because they are following the teachings of the parable of the talents or they might decide to go somewhere where many people do not help such as some parts of Eastern Europe. An example would be people helping to build or renovate an orphanage.

(e) 'Religious people should always help others who are suffering.'
Discuss this statement. You should include different, supported points of view and a personal viewpoint. You must refer to Christianity in your answer. *(12 marks)*

Most Christians would find it very difficult to disagree with this statement. There are many teachings in the Bible, particularly in the words of Jesus, which are about helping people who are suffering such as the teaching within the Parable of the Sheep and the Goats. Christians would see helping others as one of the most important things they can do in their lives because it is based on the concept of agape. Many Christians believe that they should visit people who are imprisoned for their crimes and are suffering because they need to be shown that even though they have to be punished they can eventually be forgiven.

Most non-religious people would probably agree with the statement but would say that it is not just religious people, it should be everyone. However, there are people who think that suffering is often something that people bring on themselves and therefore they should solve their own problems. They may also feel that some people should suffer if they have led bad lives and hurt others.

I am a Christian and I agree with the statement completely – I do not know how any Christian could let other people suffer if there was anything at all that they could do to help.

Examiner's comments:
These are all good answers. In particular, the responses to (d) and (e) show careful thought and consideration of the issues involved and have been supported where needed with specific teachings and examples.

Topic 4 Religion, peace and justice

These answers provide an outline of how you could construct your response. For the higher mark answers you should add your own specific examples and Bible teachings, which should be explained to show your understanding (see pages 3–4 for more guidance on this).

(a) What is capital punishment? *(1 mark)*

Capital punishment is putting someone to death for their crimes.

(b) Give two of the conditions for a 'just war'. *(2 marks)*

The war must be declared by a recognised authority. The war must have the aim to defeat evil and replace it with good.

(c) Describe Christian views on the aims of punishment. *(3 marks)*

The four aims of punishment are deterrence, protection, retribution and reformation. Most Christians would agree with deterrence, protection and reformation because they are within the Christian focus on agape but they might think that retribution is not a proper aim of punishment, as they should be forgiving as Jesus taught and not hurting others as might happen with 'an eye for an eye'.

(d) Explain how Christians might respond to social injustice. *(6 marks)*

Christians are opposed to any type of social injustice and would want to try to prevent people being discriminated against or being treated wrongly because it is against the Christian teachings of concern and love for others – agape. Many Christians take positive action against social injustice by joining organisations which fight for social equality. They might choose to give money or time to groups such as the Howard League for Prison Reform, Amnesty International or organisations such as Mencap which work to help disadvantaged people. These actions would follow the teachings of the Parable of the Sheep and the Goats.

In countries with very corrupt governments they might work to support priests who are involved with liberation theology and are trying to bring justice to the poor because Jesus came to earth to help the oppressed.

(e) 'Criminals should be punished, not forgiven.' Discuss this statement. You should include different, supported points of view and a personal viewpoint. You must refer to Christianity in your answer. *(12 marks)*

There are many people who would agree with this statement. They might argue that prison sentences should be longer and that the death penalty should be reintroduced for some crimes because the crime rate is rising and a lot of people seem to get away with doing bad actions.

However, Jesus taught forgiveness, saying that people should be forgiven 'seventy times seven times'. He said that people who repented their crimes should always be forgiven so that they had a chance to live better lives. While some Christians might think that this should be interpreted as never punishing people, most would say that some form of punishment is often necessary in order to stop people committing crimes and to protect others. They might also say that punishment gives criminals time to reform and to ask God for forgiveness.

I do not like the idea of punishment and particularly I do not believe the death penalty should ever be used but I do think that there needs to be some punishment for crime otherwise society could become completely lawless. I am a Christian and I do think that Christians should work to help people reform and follow in the footsteps of Elizabeth Fry and John Howard.

Examiner's comments:
These are very good and thoughtful answers to quite demanding questions. The responses demonstrate a range of views and are well argued and supported.

Topic 5 Religion and equality

These answers provide an outline of how you could construct your response. For the higher mark answers you should add your own specific examples and Bible teachings, which should be explained to show your understanding (see pages 3–4 for more guidance on this).

(a) What is meant by 'prejudice'? *(1 mark)*

Prejudice is an opinion, usually against someone, based on ignorance.

(b) Give two examples of discrimination. *(2 marks)*

Racism, abusive behaviour to someone of a different race, and sexism, the belief that one gender is superior to the other, are two examples of discrimination which is unfair treatment of someone.

(c) Describe how some Christians are working towards ecumenism. *(3 marks)*

Ecumenism is the breaking down of barriers between different denominations and different religions. Although most Christians are members of particular groups or denominations there are often joint services held to work towards ecumenism. There are also places such as Taizé which are ecumenical centres where Christians from different denominations come together. Some denominations or different faiths will join together in a charity project such as running youth clubs.

(d) Explain Christian teaching about the role of women in the Church. *(6 marks)*

In the New Testament there appear to be different teachings about the role of women in the Church. Jesus always seemed to treat women and men equally, such as in the story of Martha and Mary. In Corinthians Paul says that women must be silent in church and must keep their heads covered. However, in other epistles it seems that there were women leaders such as Priscilla in the Church, which would suggest that they were considered to be as important as men.

In the nineteenth century women became ministers in some nonconformist churches. Women could not become priests in the Church of England until the second half of the twentieth century and can still not be bishops. The Roman Catholic and Orthodox churches will not ordain women because they consider that the role of the priest is purely for men as Jesus was a man.

Many people argue that women should not be ordained because one of the most important parts of a priest's work is to represent Jesus when

he celebrates the Eucharist. They do not believe that this can or should be done by a woman.

(e) 'All people must be treated equally.' Discuss this statement. You should include different, supported points of view and a personal viewpoint. You must refer to Christianity in your answer. *(12 marks)*

Paul taught in his letter to the Galatians that all people were equal in Christ. Many Christians see this as really meaning that all people are equal and should be treated equally, not just Christians. Yet other Christians have interpreted this statement to mean that only Christians should be treated equally.

In fact the majority of Christians and of non-religious people would probably agree with the statement and would work to try to ensure that people are treated equally.

However, some people would say that criminals such as paedophiles and others do not deserve to be treated equally. On the other hand there are people who would argue that some people need to be treated differently because of, for example, disabilities which mean they need more help in their lives.

I am not a Christian and therefore the teachings of the Church and the Bible do not matter to me. However, I think that it is one of the most important human rights that all people should be treated equally and I also think that there is a need to give special help to people such as the disabled who might otherwise not have the opportunity to be equal.

> **Examiner's comments:**
> The response to (d) provides a good overview of the role of women in the Church as well as thorough explanation. In (e) the answer covers a range of different views with support and also provides a well-presented personal view.

Topic 6 Religion and the media

These answers provide an outline of how you could construct your response. For the higher mark answers you should add your own specific examples and Bible teachings, which should be explained to show your understanding (see pages 3–4 for more guidance on this).

(a) Give one example of the media. *(1 mark)*

Television is one form of media.

(b) What does 'censorship' mean? *(2 marks)*

Censorship means stopping a book from being published or a film or programme being shown because the people in charge do not want others to see it. An example would be the showing of the film 'The Da Vinci Code' because people did not agree with the ideas it expressed about Jesus.

(c) Describe how Christians might use the media. *(3 marks)*

Christians might use the media in order to tell more people about their faith in the hope that this will persuade them to convert to Christianity. There are several television 'God Channels' which do this. They might use television to bring services to people who may not be able to get to church because they are old or disabled in some way. They might also use the media just to present a Christian way of life to others in the hope that this will improve the world and make it a better place for everyone.

(d) Explain Christian attitudes towards the portrayal of sex in the media. *(6 marks)*

Some Christians are not particularly concerned about the way in which sex is shown in the media provided it is not shown or made available to children. However, most Christians feel that sex is a very special and sacred act which is part of the sacrament of marriage because in Genesis God created man and woman to be 'one flesh'. They may feel that sexual activity should not be shown in the media because it encourages casual sex and is against the teachings of Paul, who said people should 'flee from sexual immorality', and that all forms of pornography are wrong because they degrade people. This would be a misuse of the body and against the teachings of Paul that 'the body is a temple for the Holy Spirit'.

(e) 'Important religious figures such as Jesus should not be portrayed in the media.'
Discuss this statement. You should include different, supported points of view and a personal viewpoint. You must refer to Christianity in your answer. *(12 marks)*

There are some Christian denominations which would agree with this statement. They would say that Jesus was the Son of God and in the Ten Commandments it is forbidden to make 'graven images' which this would be. However, most Christians take a far more liberal view and believe that if it is done with respect there is nothing wrong with making films or even musicals about the life of Jesus, such as Mel Gibson's 'The Passion of the Christ'. However, they might not approve of something which gave a humorous or disrespectful representation of Jesus, such as 'Jerry Springer: The Opera' which showed Jesus in a nappy.

Muslims would agree entirely with this statement – they believe that it is wrong to represent Muhammad (pbuh) in any way and would apply exactly the same argument to representing Jesus. They would consider this to be shirk – putting something as equal to Allah.

I am not religious and so this does not really affect me. However, people's religious beliefs are very important to them and I think that everyone should treat them with respect.

Examiner's comments:
There are good responses to all parts of this question. In particular (c), (d) and (e) show a very good range of knowledge and understanding and ideas supported with reference to Christianity. The arguments in (e) are well made and supported.